FOUR CENTURIES AT THE LION HOTEL
Shrewsbury

About the author

John Butterworth has been a newspaper editor for 25 years and for 12 years was editor of the *Shrewsbury Chronicle*. He was also editor of weekly papers in Leek and Bromsgrove. In May 2008 he was awarded the MBE for services to journalism and charity after his newspapers raised more than £5m for local causes. John has been a Reader in the Church of England since 1994.

By the same author

Bruce's Baby (published by Henry E Walter Ltd)
Cults and New Faiths (published by Lion)
Too old at 40? (published privately)
God's Secret Listener (published by Monarch Books/Lion Hudson)

Four Centuries
at
The Lion Hotel

– *Shrewsbury* –

JOHN BUTTERWORTH

PUBLISHED BY THE AUTHOR
in association with
THE LION HOTEL, SHREWSBURY

First published in the UK in 2011
Published by John Butterworth
33 Kingston Drive, Walton, Stone,
Staffs ST15 0JH

ISBN 978 0 9508137 1 4

British Library Cataloguing Data
A catalogue record for this book is available from the British Library

Book design and production for the publisher by
Bookprint Creative Services, <www.bookprint.co.uk>

CONTENTS

FOREWORD BY GERALD DICKENS
Great, great grandson of Charles Dickens

THERE IS SOMETHING VERY EXCITING about visiting a building where my great, great grandfather, Charles Dickens, stayed. That experience is made even more special when there are well documented accounts of his visits. John Butterworth's wonderful history of The Lion Hotel takes that pleasure to a new level!

John's extensive local knowledge and passion for his subject is evident in every sentence, and as I read and re-read this amazing book I couldn't help smiling. As I read I felt part of every event and every anecdote, for this is certainly no dusty, academic collection of facts; it is a living, breathing, exciting addition to the rich history of an extraordinary building and town.

Many of the stories have positively Dickensian overtones: John Ashby, the man who built the current hotel, could be straight from a Dickens novel – a kind-hearted, generous and entrepreneurial host, secretly mired in crippling debt.

The hilarious spat between *The Eddowes Journal* and the *Shrewsbury Chronicle* over Jenny Lind's concert is straight from the *Pickwick Papers*, while the room at The Lion Hotel in which Dickens himself stayed could be taken from David Copperfield, with its '. . . windows bulging into the street as if they were the stern windows of a ship.' However, even Charles Dickens could never invent a character as eccentric as Mad Jack Mytton!

It is so important to collect and to re-tell the rich history around us and we should be eternally grateful to John for sharing his research with us.

I hope that you enjoy reading this account as much as I: I have no doubt that you will!

Gerald Dickens
Abingdon, Oxfordshire. 2011

PREFACE

I HAVE ONLY TWO MEMORIES of coming to Shrewsbury as a youngster, one happy and one not so happy.

The first time was in May 1961 when my dad, mum and I arrived at the Church of England Children's Society home to pick up my new sister, who was just six weeks old.

The second time was the unhappy one when my Dad and I, both Rochdale fans, went to Shrewsbury to see them beat the Dale 1-0 on a cold Saturday afternoon on January 31, 1970.

My third visit was a much longer and happier occasion when I arrived in February 1997 to be editor of the *Shrewsbury Chronicle*, one of the oldest weekly paid-for papers in the country. I was editor for 12 years and I fell in love with the place, the people and the history.

The Lion Hotel, which is just up from the River Severn, played an important part in my time at the *Chronicle* as I attended many events there. One of the highlights was appearing with the then Chief Executive of Shrewsbury and Atcham Borough Council, Robin Hooper, in a play I had written for the Shrewsbury Summer Season in 2007.

Called *A Bridge Too Far* it was the true story of the demolition in 1795 of the first Welsh Bridge, the re-building of the new one and the ensuing problems as told by Thomas Wood, the first editor of the *Chronicle*, and the Town Clerk at the time, Thomas Loxdale. I played the part of Thomas Wood while Robin Hooper was Thomas Loxdale.

Amazingly, we had a full house in the Ballroom on Thursday, June 7 to watch my amateurish attempts to be an actor and an old editor.

When I left the paper in February 2008 I had no hesitation in choosing The Lion Ballroom as my farewell evening for what was another moving occasion.

It was 18 months later when I returned to Shrewsbury for the launch of a book I had just written that I bumped into the owner of the hotel, Howard Astbury.

He mentioned the idea of writing a book on the history of The Lion and I jumped at the opportunity, and six months later this is it.

I am grateful to so many people who have helped and encouraged me on the project.

I would like to thank all the staff at Shropshire Records Office who have been so patient and helpful with all my many requests. I have been in there so often it has almost become a second home.

Also to local historian David Trumper and freelance photographer Richard Bishop who have provided practically all the excellent pictures.

Thanks go to historians Bill Champion, Barrie Trinder, Jrschina Williams-Karesch, Steve Booth and Philip Leason; Andrew Wright at St Julian's Centre; town guide Stan Sedman; Town Crier Martin Wood; writers Chris Eldon-Lee and Marjorie Dunham; Shropshire Council Business Development Manager Jon King; Shropshire Council Tourism Officer Alison Patrick; the former Arts Development Officer at Shrewsbury and Atcham Borough Council Maggie Love; and my colleague at Shropshire Newspapers, Mike Robinson, who all provided valuable support and information.

I am also very grateful to the *Shropshire Star* and the *Shrewsbury Chronicle* who published my letter to their readers asking for memories of The Lion Hotel, and *Shropshire Life* for their help. I had replies from all over the county and many told me their fascinating stories including Jancis Maloney; John Holding; Gary Harrigan; Pam Williams, who is front of house manager at The Lion; Margaret Hayes; Kenneth Clinton; Gerald Cattle and John R Brown.

I must also mention Tony Bywater, of Salop Leisure, who was a great supporter and encouragement for the project plus Dr Stuart Roberts who read the proofs for the book and, of course, Howard Astbury and all his family who were all so accommodating and patient in backing the project.

I must give a special thanks to Gerald Dickens, the great, great grandson of Charles Dickens, who has supported the project and has written the Foreword.

My final thanks go to my wife, Jan, who has lived the book with me during the last six months and has given many constructive comments and ideas.

As Editor, I soon learnt you tried to do the best job within the deadline and the resources available. It is true of this project as well. Any errors I accept are totally mine and I know there must be parts of the story I have missed out which I am sure readers will wish to tell me about.

If readers email me at john@jbutterworth.plus.com I will ensure any errors and omissions will be put right in the second edition.

1

THE GUESTS AND GHOSTS OF CHRISTMAS PAST

IF HOTELS ARE JUDGED ON THEIR GUEST LIST then The Lion in Shrewsbury has to be up with the best in Britain.

Charles Dickens, Charles Darwin, Benjamin Disraeli, Niccolo Paganini and King William IV are a few of the many names from the past who have stayed here.

And, in more recent times The Beatles, Morecambe and Wise, Cliff Richard and the Shadows, Jimmy Savile, Lulu, and Coronation Street stars Elsie Tanner and Len Fairclough are some of the celebrities who have visited the hotel.

As the *Shrewsbury Chronicle* said in its May 14 edition of 1817 when The Lion was put up for sale: 'No house upon any of the great roads between Holyhead, Bath, Cheltenham, Bristol, Liverpool, Manchester, North and South Wales stands in higher estimation (than The Lion) having a constant influx of the first families in the kingdom.'

Standing strategically at the top of Wyle Cop for at least the last four centuries, and probably much longer, The Lion has been at the centre of Shrewsbury life for many, many years.

Visitors can sense the history as they enter this grand building. They can be part of its past staying in the same rooms as Charles Dickens who described them as 'the strangest little rooms, the ceilings of which I can touch with my hand'. They can see the same windows, which the writer says, 'bulge out over the street as if they were little stern windows of a ship'. And guests can step out on to the same balcony of which Dickens wrote 'a door opens out of the sitting room on to a little open gallery with plants in it where one leans over a queer old rail'.

Residents can also dine in The Hayward Restaurant, named after the famous 19th century Shrewsbury stagecoach driver, Sam Hayward.

They can visit the 18th century Ballroom or Assembly Room, which has changed little over the centuries since Prince William of Gloucester, later King William IV, attended a ball there in 1803, or where the famous Italian musician Niccolo Paganini gave a concert there in 1833.

The architectural scholar and writers, Sir Nikolaus Pevsner and John Newman, have described it as 'an amazing room, of priceless value to the student and lover of art, and to see it alone is well worth a pilgrimage to The Lion'.

While visitors sip coffee in front of the lounge fire, or drink at the bar, they can reflect on the many famous people who have preceded them over the centuries. These include the eccentric MP for Shrewsbury, John 'Mad Jack' Mytton, who rather than come through the main door to The Lion, preferred to jump in through one of the windows, leaving a shower of glass behind him.

Outside, people can see where Charles Darwin caught the stagecoach to London at the front door to join HMS Beagle and begin his epic voyage of discovery.

They can look at the entrance to The Lion, considerably widened for modern cars, where a crowd would gather to watch Sam Hayward gallop up Wyle Cop with the Wonder stagecoach, nicknamed the Yellow Belly. At the top of the road he would turn full circle to enter The Lion's yard at speed, having only inches to spare on either side, much to the horror of any travellers on top who had never been on the Wonder before.

They can also see the balcony from where Benjamin Disraeli, who went on to be Prime Minister twice, gave his victory speech after being elected MP for Shrewsbury during the bitter 1841 election campaign.

Residents can look up at the famous stone lion above the front door, which dominates the hotel, and which the owners used as a logo in their advertisements on the front page of the *Shrewsbury Chronicle*, one of the oldest weekly newspapers in Britain, to advertise the stagecoaches that left The Lion in the 18th and 19th centuries.

Leaving the hotel, residents can explore Shrewsbury, which has probably the biggest number of black and white buildings in the country, and follow in the footsteps of fellow guest Charles Dickens who gave readings of *A Christmas Carol* at the Music Hall. They can still see where Darwin lived on The Mount, where he went to the original Shrewsbury School (now the town library) and worshipped and preached at the Unitarian Church a couple of hundred yards away from The Lion.

Join the many hundreds of famous people, including King Aethelred, King Edward I, King Edward II, Prince Rupert, King Henry II, King Henry IV, King Charles I, Queen Victoria, Charles Wesley, Daniel Defoe and Robert Clive, plus many others who have visited Shrewsbury.

But first, take a guided tour through history at The Lion itself, and meet some of its many famous guests – and ghosts.

2

GOING BACK TO THE FOURTEENTH CENTURY

ONE OF THE EARLIEST RECORDS of The Lion appeared in the *Shrewsbury Chronicle* in its November 29, 1777, edition.

Tucked away on page three in the middle of a column underneath the imaginative headline, 'Shrewsbury, Nov 29', the paper reports: 'Last week was erected, over the new and elegant Assembly Room, at The Lion Inn in this town, on a beautiful pedestal, decorated with the arms of John Ashby Esq., a highly finished statue of a lion, larger than life, executed by Mr John Nelson, statuary carver, of this place. This statue, and another of the same size and elegance, do great credit we think to the artist, as well as to the generous and public spirited employer.' That is the entire *Chronicle* report. But it helps local historians to credit John Nelson, a celebrated Shrewsbury stone-carver, as the craftsman responsible for the statues and to show the hotel owner then was Shrewsbury solicitor John Ashby (1722-1779), who was Mayor of Shrewsbury from 1759-60 and town clerk from 1767 until his death 12 years later.

Incidentally, both the lions can still be seen today, although the rear lion only re-emerged in 1962 after a hotel extension was built.

Shrewsbury carpenter and joiner William Haycock, who rebuilt The Lion, said that Ashby bought the premises, described in the deeds as the 'Red Lion', at auction in August 1775 from Sir Thomas Jones, of Stanley Hall, near Bridgnorth. And it was Ashby who renamed it The Lion.

However, the history of the hotel, or The Lion site, goes back much further.

There is a conversation recorded 'at the sign of the Lion' in 1537 between Nicholas Holte; John Barber, Richard Owen's father; and Thomas Cowper, for many years the town clerk of the borough. They were discussing rumours that the King (Henry VIII) was planning to halve the number of churches, as part of the English Reformation, and to have only one chalice in each church.

Historian Bill Champion says in *Shropshire History and Archaeology Volume LXXV*, that, although the reference is only to The Lion, there is no doubt that the Red Lion is meant.

The first recorded owner of the Red Lion was Richard Mytton Esq. (c. 1500-

1591) who sold it in May 1553 to the sitting tenant Richard Owen, alias Barber, for £20 and a fixed fee-farm rent of 12 shillings (60p) per year. Selling in fee-farm was an old type of conveyance whereby the vendor would sell the freehold, but retain a fixed annual rent called a 'fee-farm'.

However, Mr Champion believes the present hotel site had belonged to the Myttons since 1460, and probably earlier. The Myttons were one of the most famous Shropshire families who made their fortunes in the 14th century in the wool trade.

Richard's grandfather, Thomas Mytton, is best remembered for the story, possibly apocryphal, that in August 1485 when Henry Tudor decided to cross from Wales into England at Shrewsbury on his way to do battle with Richard III at Bosworth Field, Thomas Mytton refused to let him over the Welsh Bridge, saying: 'We know no King but Richard, Henry Tudor shall not enter this town but over my belly,' i.e. over his dead body.

However, after seeing Henry's large army and following advice from colleagues he decided it was more prudent to let Henry into Shrewsbury. So as not to lose face, Mytton lay in the road on the Welsh Bridge 'belly upward' for Henry to step over him.

The royal visitor is believed to have stayed at Tudor House, which is still there on Wyle Cop below The Lion, before marching to Bosworth where King Richard III was killed. Henry became Henry VII, ending the War of the Roses and beginning the Tudor dynasty.

Mr Champion says that deeds for the adjoining property uphill from The Lion on Wyle Cop show that the site of The Lion had been owned by Thomas's grandfather, Richard Mytton, by 1399 at least.

Incidentally, Richard Mytton was a leading London wool exporter, who had been indicted in 1413 for defrauding his Shropshire suppliers. He had also been fined in 1406 at the Shrewsbury Great Court for blocking the 'Wyle' with trees, possibly a reference to the rebuilding needed after a devastating fire had destroyed Wyle Cop in 1393.

These dates would fit in with the tradition that Prince Hal, who was Harry the Prince of Wales and son of the Lancastrian King Henry IV, lodged at the Red Lion after the Battle of Shrewsbury on July 21, 1403.

The Prince, who was injured in the battle, continued to help his father defeat the rebels, who were led by Henry 'Hotspur' Percy from Northumberland.

If Shakespeare is to be believed the young Prince enjoyed 'hot wenches in flame coloured taffeta' and was the despair of his father with his frequent visits to local taverns.

☐   ☐   ☐

Meanwhile, when Ashby died on January 29, 1779, he left with a fine reputation but with his financial affairs in a state of great confusion. The *Shrewsbury Chronicle* reported that: 'He was a gentleman, whose exemplary virtues and amiable qualities are a more lasting monument of his good name, than any eulogy can express.'

However, his finances were not exemplary, and it was thanks to the papers from the ensuing litigation that much can be pieced together about Ashby and the story of The Lion at that time.

One of the most important creditors was the carpenter and joiner William Haycock, who said Ashby had employed him in September 1775 to take down the Red Lion 'and to erect a New House on the same spot called the Lion Inn'.

Haycock said he had then 'proceeded to erect the New Building and, in the course of the business, frequent alterations were made and great enlargements of the House in consequence of the said John Ashby's determination of building a large Assembly Room (or Ballroom) with a Card Room adjoining and a Dining Room under the Assembly Room, and other additional rooms were made in order to be convenient and subservient to the Assembly Room.'

Haycock's bill for rebuilding The Lion was just over £2,698 and he claimed £965 was still owed by Ashby's estate. (For more details of the many other traders owed money for helping build The Lion see Appendix 2).

According to the records, dismantling the old Red Lion began at the end of September 1775 and it seems Ashby allowed work to proceed as and when finances were available.

Haycock was responsible for the overall design of the Assembly Room, as shown by his letter, dated May 9, 1777, which he sent to Ashby's London address at the Crown Coffee House, Covent Garden.

Sir,

I have sent as you desir'd a Drawing of the Ball and Drawing Roome, and hope they will be inteligable enough for your workmen to understand them, you have mented in your letter to me of having ornaments provided! The plaister ornaments are shown on two of the peirs in the drawing, they are on the chimney side and on the peirs in the circular end: are now under hand, so that no ornaments will be wanting for the peirs. Likewise in the same letter you mention'd your having 3 branches of cast brass, those must be lacker'd and in 3 or 4 years' time, will get very black and dirty. If you could have them of iron, or any metal that could be jappan'd, they will be easily clean'd, or if painted, are soon renew'd.

We are getting on with the Joyners' work as fast as we can. Miss Elisha gave us possession of her stable on Tuesday last, we have almost finish'd getting down the old Malthouse.

Am Sir Your Humble Servt Willem Haycock

Early in 1778, the new Lion was ready and Ashby appointed John Richards as the innkeeper on March 21, 1778, the same day the opening was advertised in the *Shrewsbury Chronicle*.

The first event held in the Assembly Room on Thursday, November 12, 1778, was the Shrewsbury Hunt Ball, and no expense was spared.

In the 1770s, the Hunt Week in November had become one of the main social events in the county calendar.

And for Ashby, who maintained a huntsman and a pack of 38 hounds at his county seat at the Lynches, Yockleton, it was a fitting coup to win this leading social event off his rival, the Raven & Bell.

The Hunt President and friend of Ashby, George Forrester of Willey, revealed that £83 was spent on the occasion.

There were three dozen bottles of wine, 49 bottles of port, 27 bottles of Madeira, 15 bottles of old hock, five bottles of claret, 18 bottles of cider, as well as ale and porter, a dark brown liquor. They even included two guineas to cover the cost of smashed glasses and china.

Despite the success of The Lion, Ashby, who had been described as a shrewd, entrepreneurial lawyer and 'a guardian of many secrets', was living beyond his means.

When Ashby, who was married but had no children, died all his £31,000 debts came to light and the ensuing problems took more than ten years to sort out.

One of the claims was by the trustees of the late Robert Clive of India, who had died in 1774. They said they were owed £12,000, which Ashby had collected as receiver of the rents from the Clive estates in Shropshire.

Mr Champion believes that Ashby had probably used the Clive money to help finance the re-building of The Lion.

As a result, there was another big, but not so happy social event at The Lion on Friday, October 8, 1779, just one year after opening, when a grand sale was held of all the owner's goods, including a 'considerable' cellar, to help pay off his bills. It lasted an incredible 14 days.

A magnificent sales catalogue, printed by the Shrewsbury firm of Eddowes,

The old entrance to the Lion Hotel. Notice how much smaller it is compared to the new entrance. But it was through this narrow gap that Sam Hayward would bring the Shrewsbury Wonder stagecoach at full speed with only a couple of inches to spare on either side. This picture was taken around 1895. [Picture supplied by David Trumper]

A more modern picture of The Lion taken circa 1950. Notice how much wider the entrance is compared to the 1895 picture. [Picture supplied by David Trumper]

Looking back from the hotel car park for a different view of the old archway. Notice the marks from the stagecoach wheels can be seen at the bottom of the left hand column. [Picture: Richard Bishop]

After filming A Christmas Carol *in Shrewsbury in 1984 all the props were taken away apart from this 'gravestone' of Ebenezer Scrooge which can still be seen in St Chad's churchyard today.*

This picture, dated April 29, 1953, shows William Braddock, a local decorator for Edwin Coles, putting the gold leaf on the lion over the hotel door. The lion, which was the work of local sculptor John Nelson, was erected in 1777. [Picture supplied by David Trumper]

The Lion Hotel around 1922 with the coal merchant Breeze Ltd next door. [Picture supplied by David Trumper]

The Charles Darwin statue that split a town. While the council were debating putting up this statue a gale blew down the top 50ft of St Mary's Church spire on Sunday, February 11, 1894, which the then vicar, the Rev Newdegate Poyntz, said was divine retribution.

An old drawing of the back of The Lion hangs in the hotel reception. [Picture: Richard Bishop]

A large dramatic old picture of The Lion Hotel and Wyle Cop, dating from circa 1890, hangs above the fireplace in the tapestry lounge. [Picture: Richard Bishop]

The back of The Lion and the garage around 1925. [Picture supplied by David Trumper]

At the staff party in 1958 are, from the left, Kenneth Clinton, Mrs Edwards, the head waiter's wife; Mrs Jones, the hotel manageress; Major Jones the manager and Leslie Hutchinson, hotel pianist.

The Severn Valley Motoring Club enjoy their dinner at The Lion in 1957.

provides a detailed picture of a well-stocked inn and survives in the Chancery Masters' Exhibits, giving the names of purchasers and prices paid.

The sales catalogue gives an insight into The Lion, which was listed as having kitchens, servants' hall and quarters, parlours, larders, cellars and butler's pantry plus 10 chambers, 5 lodging rooms, 3 dining rooms, the Assembly Room, card and coffee rooms adjoining and 2 bars. There was even a small fire engine kept in the garden.

The town and country gentry enjoyed the social occasion and the rich pickings from the sale, which raised £1,508 from furnishings and £376 from the sale of Ashby's extensive library, but that was nowhere near enough to pay off the debts.

According to the *London Gazette*, £9,222 was then realised by the sale of Ashby's personal estate.

But more money was needed, so Ashby's manor at Yockleton was sold for £12,000 and The Lion and some of the adjoining premises, including Sycamore House, the octagonal building at the rear of The Lion Hotel which Ashby had left in his will to his wife and which can still be seen today, were sold for £1,000 to Shrewsbury stationer John Bishop, who was town mayor in 1790.

☐   ☐   ☐

More light is shed on Ashby's problems by the local historian, the Rev Hugh Owen, who had been vicar of St Julian's since 1791 and who had The Lion in his parish.

Writing in the early 19th century he said: 'As long as Mr Ashby lived, The Lion was esteemed one of the most comfortable as well as most handsome large inns in England.'

He said that when Mr Ashby died there were 'involved circumstances' from the 'expense he had incurred in the building and management of this inn, with a general, liberal, elegant and hospitable manner of life'.

The vicar added: 'His affairs fell into the hands of a Mr Morgan, his partner and head clerk, by whose delay and mismanagement the creditors were long kept from their just claims.'

Just 18 months after re-opening, The Lion was stripped bare and it was left vacant for a year before being taken on in the autumn of 1780 by Robert Lawrence who found it in a sad and sorry state of repair.

The Rev Owen said The Lion was bought by the creditors of a company of gentlemen 'who successfully sold their shares one by one to the tenant Lawrence who made a good fortune by his coaches'.

However, thanks to Lawrence's hard work and the booming stagecoach business the hotel was about to gallop into a golden era.

3

A JOLTING JOURNEY FROM THE LION TO LONDON

I F PEOPLE THINK TODAY'S ROADS ARE BAD for potholes they are nothing compared to the days when stagecoaches set off on a jolting journey from The Lion Hotel to London, Wales and Ireland.

The ancient problem of maintaining the highways was tackled by Tudor legislation in the 16th century. The Statute of Bridges of 1531 said bridges were to be repaired by local inhabitants while the Highways Act of 1555 said the parishes were responsible for maintaining the roads. All parishioners had to work unpaid for four consecutive days, later increased to six, on an annual basis. They were expected to bring their own pick, shovel and cart and were supervised by two Surveyors of the Highways, who were also unpaid.

Unsurprisingly, the system was not a great success. The parishioners did as little work as possible, filling in a few holes caused by heavy wagons for a couple of hours, then concentrated on the by-ways which led to their own fields before retiring to the local tavern for the rest of the day.

Progress with transport was not really made until the 18th century Turnpike Bills, which transferred the cost of the roads' upkeep from the parish to the road users, so all who used the road, apart from the Army and Navy, had to stop and pay at the toll house gates. Not everyone took kindly to this road tax, such as farmers going to market, and George II was compelled to make pulling down a toll gate a punishable offence after tempers frayed and fights broke out over payment.

The quality of road building and surfaces were improved and Shrewsbury's inns saw the business opportunity, so in 1750 set up a weekly wagon service between Shrewsbury and Chester. Called a People Carrier the wagon was fitted on either side with benches carrying 12 or more passengers, replacing the clumsier and slower stage-wagons.

Up until then, people had previously travelled either by foot, on horseback or by boat to Bristol to catch the ocean going ships.

However, as early as 1681 there are records of a wagon service from Shropshire to London via Wellington and Newport Pagnell. But to show how unsafe it was that same year a gang of nine robbed the passengers – it was later found that three of them were women dressed as men.

In April 1753, the first regular weekly and direct public transport service from Shrewsbury to London was launched from the Red Lion, the forerunner to The Lion. Called the *Birmingham and Shrewsbury Long Coach with six able horses* it took four days with a ticket costing 18 shillings (90p) one way. Until then it had meant travelling to Coventry and Oxford to connect with a coach to London.

Later new coach models were introduced, such as The Machine and the New Fly, which were built with special steel springs for extra comfort, and by 1773 the time taken to get to London was reduced to two days, which included an overnight stay in Oxford.

In the 1780s, services from Shrewsbury to Bath and Bristol were established via Worcester and Cheltenham, followed in later years with coaches to Manchester, Chester and Exeter.

In 1835, 23 coaches ran in total from Shrewsbury, with 15 of them starting from The Lion. Seven of those went to London, while there was also a daily mail coach to Chester, Hereford, Welshpool and Newtown and coaches to Barmouth and Aberystwyth, which had become popular sea bathing resorts.

In those days, it was said 200 coach horses were accommodated in Shrewsbury every night and grooms could be seen washing the travel-stained animals in shallower parts of the town's River Severn.

Travellers could either travel inside the coaches, or pay half price and sit outside on thinly padded seats with an iron rail as the only backrest.

Sitting on top, particularly at night, could be dangerous, if not fatal, if the person nodded off and hadn't tied himself to the metal handrail, hence the meaning of the phrase dropping off.

That wasn't the only problem, it could be bitterly cold and inside passengers, who were given bales of straw to help them sleep, often complained of being kept awake by the stamping feet of passengers on the roof trying to stay warm.

On Christmas Day, 1836, when the stagecoach reached Bath after heavy snow on the way, the innkeeper wondered why the three outside passengers didn't get up from their seats. It took him some time to realise they couldn't move – because they had all frozen to death.

Another problem for passengers was getting meals on the way as they would be allowed only about 25 minutes at stops such as The Lion to eat.

When the stagecoach was ready to depart a bell would ring and it would set off – even if all the passengers weren't on board.

But on summer days it was a very pleasant form of transport. In 1808, prolific writer and poet Robert Southey wrote about his travel in a stagecoach around the country from a foreigner's perspective in his *Letters from England,* under the pseudonym, Don Manuel Alvarez Aspriella (presumably the 19th century equivalent to Bill Bryson). Travelling on top of a stagecoach, he said: 'The sun was setting and the long twilight of an English summer evening gave to the English landscape a charm wholly of its own. As soon as it grew dark, the coach lamps were lighted. Starlight and mild summer air made the situation most agreeable. Life has not many things better than this.'

Although in the main black horses were used to pull the stagecoaches there was one grey horse that achieved notoriety. On June 6, 1798, the *Salopian Journal* reported that: 'Mr Lawrence, of The Lion Hotel, in this town in September 1784, purchased a grey horse that was five years old and used to run the mail. This extraordinary animal, now 19 years old, continues to perform this severe duty six days every week with wonderful spirit and activity, and from correct calculation it appears that between September 1784 and September 1796 he has travelled with his vehicle of upward 77,000 miles.'

▢ ▢ ▢

Although the London route was by far the most lucrative, it was the London–Shrewsbury–Dublin mail connection that brought most benefit to the town.

That was the brainchild of Robert Lawrence, the then owner of The Lion, who was hugely influential in ensuring the prosperity of the town and his hotel. The former owner of the Raven & Bell Hotel, who had moved to The Lion in 1780 taking his business with him, sought out local landowners to convince them the project would be a success and encouraged the upper servants in noble houses to set up inns along the road. Travelling via Wrexham, Mold, St Asaph and Conway, the service, launched in July 1779, ran three times a week with a journey time of one and a half days and a fare of £2 and two shillings (£2.10). When the Lord Lieutenant of Ireland, Earl Temple, arrived at The Lion for an official reception on September 3, 1782, on the new coach, he was said to be extremely glad that the Shrewsbury road had been recommended to him as he found it 'not only considerably nearer but the accommodations were in every respect perfectly to his satisfaction'.

When he said he would use this route regularly it was the equivalent to The Lion and Shrewsbury getting a Royal seal of approval. Soon a slightly changed route was opened via Oswestry, Corwen and Llanrwst to Conway.

Shrewsbury's part on the coaching route between London and Holyhead figured even more in1801 when the Anglo Irish Act of Union abolished the Dublin Parliament and centralised government in Westminster. To ensure this important route was not jeopardised, Lawrence hired people to clear the snow and formed a landlords' association so each of them was responsible for keeping their part of the road in good condition. It is largely because of Lawrence that The Lion became one of the most celebrated coaching inns in the country in the late 18th century. He also ensured that Shrewsbury became the local centre for travellers, traders and stagecoaches – rather than Chester.

In Minshull's guide to Shrewsbury of 1803 it was stated that 'of late years this town has been a principal thoroughfare between London, Birmingham, Bristol and Dublin, through the perseverance of Mr Lawrence'.

However, Shrewsbury nearly lost the important Dublin route in 1809 when Sir Henry Parnell, a top Government official, threatened to withdraw all mail coaches from using the Shrewsbury–Holyhead route because of the dangerous state of some of the roads.

North Wales had been described as 'full of bad roads and bad inns and uncertain fords' – many cottages still had no glass windows, only wicker windows.

To solve the problem Parliament decided to commission Thomas Telford to build a new road to Holyhead. A grant of £20,000 was provided and Telford made it a condition that only professional surveyors and skilled men should work for him. It took ten years to complete and when finished in 1819, one member of the House of Commons described it as 'the finest highway in the world'. Today that road is known as the A5.

Lawrence was also responsible for a big change to The Lion when in 1793/94 he took on the property below, No. 75 Wyle Cop, and used it as a post office.

On September 7, 1806, Robert Lawrence died aged 57. In a tribute, the *Salopian Journal* reported:

Died last Wednesday after a long illness, which he bore with becoming fortitude, Mr Robert Lawrence, formerly of the Raven & Bell and late of The Lion Inn, in this town, whose social qualities and cheerful manners through life greatly endeared him to a very large circle of friends and acquaintances. By the extensive capacity and solid judgement of this enterprising young man, the great road from London to Holyhead was first planned and first effected by his zeal and exertions and during a period of upward 40 years the communication between the United Kingdom of Great Britain and Ireland has been much accelerated and improved, and to him the public are considerably indebted for the great facility and expectation with which travellers are now conveyed through this part of the country.

His memorial inside St Julian's Church, only a few yards away from The Lion, says: 'To the memory of Mr Robert Lawrence, many years proprietor of the Raven and Lion inns in this town, to whose public spirit and unremitting exertions for upwards of 30 years in opening of the great road thro' Wales between the united kingdoms the public in general have been greatly indebted and will long have to regret his loss.'

His remains were interred in the ancient church at Battlefield, near Shrewsbury.

To show how much Lawrence and the others achieved; in February 1730 it took a party of three ladies, five gentlemen and six servants 12 days to travel from Shrewsbury to London.

By the mid 1820s this had been cut to 16 hours, thanks mainly to Sam Hayward.

4

SAM HAYWARD – HE DROVE THE FASTEST STAGECOACH IN THE WEST

THE MOST CELEBRATED OF ALL The Lion drivers was Samuel 'Sam' Hayward, who ran the Shrewsbury Wonder coach for 16 years without mishap and was a legend on the route to London.

Born in Ellesmere in 1805, the coachman was never more than 10 minutes late in all the years he drove the Wonder. He was helped by Isaac Taylor, who ran the coaching business at The Lion. Taylor dominated the coaching scene in Shrewsbury in the 19th century just as Lawrence had done in the 18th century.

It was said of Taylor: 'Such a character for regularity the coach (the Wonder) could never have obtained without good horses, good coachmen and good tackle and they were indebted to these to the coach proprietor. Mr Taylor was one of the first to accommodate the public in this excellent manner.'

Taylor had come from an inn-keeping family, with his father keeping the Haygate at Wellington and his brother looking after the Jerningham Arms at Shifnal. He was confident he could deliver a first class service as his advertisement in 1834 predicted he would 'at all times be desirous of having sufficient first-rate coaches to all the great commercial towns and fashionable watering-places in England, so as to prevent the public from experiencing that inconvenience and delay they would meet with a second-rate establishment'.

It was quite a spectacle when the Wonder, nicknamed the 'yellow belly' because of its colour, left The Lion at 5am for London – fare £1 inside and 10 shillings (50p) on top. It was run on military discipline and time-keeping.

In the book *Victorian Shrewsbury* it quotes a spectator who wrote: 'Before the hour all passengers were required to be in their places, all luggage had to be safely packed and as the chime of the first of the four quarters rang out from St Julian's church tower, Richard Ash, the guard, clambered to his place. The coachman took his seat on the box, and with this first stroke of the hour, the four well-groomed steeds dashed forward under the archway of the inn-yard. The horse cloths were removed with a flourish, the skid was put on as the corner was turned and sharply went the heavy vehicle down the Wyle Cop.'

The Wonder, which began in 1825, changed horses at the Haygate, Wellington, and then at the Jerningham Arms, Shifnal, where it was reported: 'A hasty snack was often taken by a hungry passenger who had not got up in time to breakfast at The Lion before punctual departure of the Wonder. It was a pretty sight to see this coach dash along the wide street of the town.'

The report continued:

The horses were piloted in splendid style by the celebrated Sam Hayward, whose stolid-looking face was scarcely ever lit up by a smile, except of the grimmest, while the well-known 'Dicky' Ash, the sententious guard, gave a very feeble imitation of a popular air upon his many-keyed bugle. In an instant the narrow street opposite the Jerningham Arms was full of life and commotion; the horses were out and in again in the twinkling of an eye, as it were.

The imperturbable coachman was in his place, while Richard gave the warning in measured tones: 'Now – gentlemen – if – you – please – time – is – up'. This was all; there was no mistaking the meaning of it; and away sped the Wonder.

As Sam arrived at the bottom of the Wyle Cop, a large crowd would gather to watch the stagecoach come up to The Lion. Sam's reputation for timekeeping was so great that if the Shrewsbury market clock didn't coincide with the advertised time of the Wonder, the clock was declared to be wrong.

However, Sam was not renowned as one of the world's great conversationalists. Apparently, passengers would lay bets on whether he would utter a single word during the journey. When a passenger once asked him: 'What the deuce ails you? Are you dumb, man?' Sam replied: 'Can't drive and talk too.'

But he did once speak to a young lawyer coming to Shrewsbury for the first time, who was concerned at the steepness of Wyle Cop. At the bottom of the hill he leaned over to Hayward and said: 'I think I'll get off.'

'You be damned,' replied Sam as he hurtled up the hill, not wanting to stop and lose any vital seconds on the journey.

This was not surprising as Sam's greatest claim to fame was the speed at which he would come up Wyle Cop, turning full circle at the top to enter The Lion's yard without stopping and having only inches to spare on either side, a feat only one other coach driver ever attempted.

A writer at the time said of the spectacle: 'It never failed to draw an appreciative knot of spectators or to transfix with horror any strangers who might choose to be among the outside passengers (on the Wonder).'

Interestingly, the entrance to The Lion which visitors now go through has been widened for cars and was quite a bit narrower in Sam's day. However, the original archway is still there where the marks from Sam's wheels can be seen on one of the columns.

There was intense rivalry between the stagecoaches (Sam's brother drove the Holyhead Mail coach). In the 1830s the Wonder, and one of its rivals, the Nimrod, used to race each other, with bets being put on who would win, particularly on May Day when it became almost accepted practice that horses and riders 'were spurred on to super human and super equine exertions'. It was risky, but it certainly helped to reduce the travelling times.

What also helped the drivers were the tips, on average a florin (10p) per 50 miles. They were quite well paid with a weekly wage of between 10 and 16 shillings (50p to 80p) but with the tips the work was very lucrative.

To steal a march on their competitors The Lion would agree to pay the road tolls every month and so the turnpike gate was opened as soon as the Wonder came speeding into view almost like modern trains passing through a level crossing.

The Wonder would leave the old Bull and Mouth Inn in St Martin Le Grande, London, at 6.30am before reaching the Peacock, Islington, at 6.45am.

To show how important the journey times were Charles G Harper reproduced this original schedule for the Wonder.

Proprietors	Places	Miles	Time allowed	Should arrive
Sherman	St Albans	22 ½	2 hrs 3mins	8.48
J Lilley	Redbourne	4 ½	25 mins (Breakfast 20 mins)	9.13
Goodyear	Dunstable	8 ¼	48 mins	10.21
Sheppard	Daventry	29 ¾	2 hrs 54 mins	2.15
Collier	Coventry	19	1 hr 47 mins (Business 5 mins)	4.02
Vyse	Birmingham	19	1 hr 39 mins (Dinner 35 mins)	5.46
Evans	Wolverhampton	14	1 hr 15 mins (Business 5 mins)	7.36
Evans	Summer House	6 ½	35 mins	8.16
J Taylor	Shifnal	6 ½	35 mins	8.51
H J Taylor	Haygate	8	43 mins	9.34
I Taylor	Shrewsbury	10	56 mins	10.30

The Wonder was the first stagecoach to achieve more than 100 miles in a day. Taking out the time for stops and changing horses its average speed was 11½ mph.

But the high fares excluded many poorer travellers who had to use the slow and cumbersome stage wagons or else walk.

The nobility and gentry usually used their own horses and carriages, so it was mainly professional men, commercial travellers – and, surprisingly, foreign visitors who travelled on the stagecoaches.

When the Wonder came across an accident in 1840, its passengers included M Theophile Van de Woestyne, attaché to the Belgian Embassy; his brother and their valet; Count Pollem, the Sardinian minister and his valet; a consulting surgeon from Gloucester and three other gentlemen.

By 1838, the Wonder went only to Birmingham and not London and then in 1842 it was reduced to a two horse coach which was lamented in this verse.

> Adown the Wyle Cop, prince of coachmen, no more
> Shall you ever be seen touching up your swift four,
> But spare us, O Hayward, O spare us, forbear,
> From driving the Wonder with only a pair

After Sam retired from driving, he kept the Raven and the Bell Inn until he died in 1851. He asked to be buried in St Julian's Churchyard with a flat gravestone overlooking Wyle Cop so that he could show he was an ordinary person by allowing people to walk on his grave.

However, the Wonder and Sam Hayward are not totally forgotten.

- Sam's family still live in Shropshire. His great niece, Margaret Hayes, of Bayston Hill, said their family still talk about their famous forefather with pride. Her mother, Mrs Elizabeth Benbow, who was one of Sam's nieces and who died in 2009 aged 91, liked to take Margaret to The Lion and tell her about its coaching past.
- In 1993, Mr George Wilkins drove a 1986 replica of the Wonder with two teams of Dutch harness horses from Land's End to John o'Groats in aid of the British Heart Foundation. He left Cornwall on March 26 on the 1,000-mile trip, passed through Shrewsbury and arrived in the north of Scotland on Sunday, May 1 at 11.30am.
- The Lion Hotel has named its restaurant, The Hayward, after the driver of the Wonder.

- For those who want to see the original Wonder (accession number 1966F21) it is at the Birmingham Museum's Collections Centre in 25 Dollman Street, Duddeston, Nechells, Birmingham, B7 4RQ, which is open only on certain dates. For more details ring 0121 303 0190.

5

FIRST CLASS MAIL SERVICE

THE MOST REGAL COACH TO COME TO SHREWSBURY was the Royal Mail and crowds would watch it arrive. Described as the *King of the Road* the first mail coach service between Shrewsbury and London was launched on September 5, 1785.

Its post horn announced its coming from some distance away as the coach flew along the road, wheels crunching over the uneven cobbles and tired horses panting as they climbed the steep hill of Wyle Cop, making a colourful and noisy entrance to The Lion.

The doors and panels of the Royal Mail coaches were painted maroon, contrasting with the shiny black upper panels with the wheels painted post office red. The Royal Arms were carefully painted on the doors while the front boot of the coach, which held the passenger luggage, had the reigning King's or Queen's initials painted on them and the rear boot, which held the mail bags and the repair kit, had the number of the carriage. To cope with the water, mud and stones the wooden body of the mail coach was painted with up to an astonishing 50 coats of paint and varnish.

The mail coach was made of ash framing with deal side panel and a mahogany floor while the side panels were covered in leather and painted. Legroom was only 18.5 inches and the passengers were all given travel rugs. To ensure deadlines were met and timings were accurate the brass coach clock was locked in a mahogany case.

There was an armed guard carrying two pistols, a sword and a blunderbuss with his feet on the locked iron-clad mail box in the rear boot, access to which was through a trapdoor.

A Shrewsbury traveller described one of the guards as 'one of the most swaggering fellows I had ever encountered, a true dandy dressed in ruffles and nankeen breeches and white stockings'.

The coaching industry provided a much-needed boost to the town's economy which had been suffering since the loss of the Welsh woollen cloth trade. It gave new sources of income to innkeepers, shopkeepers and farriers and jobs to drivers, coach repairers, caterers and stable lads.

Until Tudor times, there had been no organised postal service in England. Letters were entrusted to people travelling to a certain destination or sometimes servants were sent with a message.

It was Henry VIII (1509-47) who tried to set up the first kind of national postal service organising a Master of the Posts to arrange for a relay system to carry important Government reports along designated routes.

The Monarch saw the need to send orders and receive reports, particularly during a time of war, while wealthy landowners, often living away from their estates, wanted to keep in touch with their bailiffs who were managing their land.

He took advantage of the system set up by Edward I (1239-1307) who had arranged for innkeepers placed up to 20 miles apart to be paid to have fresh horses ready for the King's Messengers.

The Latin word for placed is *positus* which was shortened to post with the innkeeper who stabled the horses becoming known as the postmaster. Setting up a line of posts was known as 'laying a post' and towns, such as Shrewsbury, benefited greatly from being on that post line. Post boys and servants on horseback were used to transport the messages.

In the 1590s the Red Lion is known to have been used as a contact point for messengers employed by the Council in the Marches at Ludlow.

As part of the innkeeper's contract with the Government, Queen Elizabeth I (1558-1603) had decreed: 'That everie poste doe keepe three horses at least contynuallie in stable bothe winter and somer, or have them so neere unto his house that the furthest he maie be ready to depart with the pacquette within one quarter of an hour after he hearth the boye or man blow his horne that bryngeth it.'

Generally, there were five horses in a team, working backwards and forwards along a route, although only four would be needed at any one time. The idea was that each horse would work hard for about one hour a day for four days, before resting on the fifth day. Coaching horses were usually well bred and, by 1835, there were approximately 150,000 horses pulling coaches in Britain.

When one London firm tried to beat its rivals by advertising average speeds of 12mph, it killed seven horses in three weeks. In the hot summer of 1821, the Wonder had to reduce its speed to keep its horses alive.

The post boys had to keep to a strict timetable to ensure the post was delivered on time. With the improvement in road surfaces from the middle of the 18th century many post boys found they could travel faster by coach than they could on horseback.

They would arrive at The Lion carrying large, heavy bags or portmanteaux which had been sealed and fastened in London and contained a ticket with the time they left the capital.

Towards the end of the 18th century the increase in mail and the continued use of post boys to deliver letters was causing problems, particularly with more money orders being sent through the post which encouraged a big rise in highwaymen and robberies.

John Palmer, a theatrical manager from Bath, first proposed to the Prime Minister, William Pitt, in the early 1780s that the nation's mail should be carried in sealed boxes on fast coaches under permanent armed guard.

Palmer was allowed to carry out trial runs at his own expense and the experiment worked so well that Pitt rewarded Palmer by appointing him Surveyor and Controller-General of the Post Office in 1786. With many out of work soldiers looking for gainful employment they took over the main routes from the post boys who were left with the minor deliveries along the byways.

The coach drivers, or artists as they were known, were extremely skilful, as Sam Hayward demonstrated.

A good artist, usually elegantly dressed in a scarlet frock coat, a white hat and kid gloves was an expert at handling the reins or 'ribbons'. His job was demanding because he often had to take control of four horses he had never seen before and was always wary of problem horses such as 'bolter' and 'jibbers'.

However, the real heroes were the Royal Mail guards who were well aware of their superior status and their seat, at the rear of the coach, was higher than the driver's. They were employed by the Royal Mail, while the drivers worked for contractors.

In an attempt to avoid bribery and corruption the guards were paid ten shillings and sixpence a week (52.5p) which was a large sum then, plus tips and a good pension.

In return, the guards were expected to risk life and limb to protect the mail. They were responsible if the coach broke down and so always carried spare chains, nails, ropes, bolts, clips for temporary wheels and bars to repair broken springs.

The repair kit was certainly needed in 1822 when a hurricane hit western Britain, causing terrible damage, uprooting many trees and blowing the Shrewsbury to Holyhead mail coach over near Capel Curig in North Wales.

On steep hills the guard was expected to jump off and place an iron drag under one of the rear wheels to slow it down.

They were also expected to be able to read and write to complete the time-sheet or way bill and to explain any delays.

They guaranteed a next day delivery, even if the mail was posted on Christmas Eve.

The Royal Mail guard would carry the famous post horn and as he approached an inn he would blow the horn to tell the inn-keeper to prepare the new set of horses. And woe betide any inn-keeper who did not have them ready on time!

Five minutes was all that was allocated to change the horses with the record at Shrewsbury being under 50 seconds.

But some guards had a sense of humour and, if they were running late, they would play songs such as 'Oh dear, what can the matter be?'

Once a Royal Mail delivery caused unexpected hustle and bustle at The Lion on December 7, 1824, when two boxes from Dublin arrived on the Holyhead coach bound for London.

When the boxes were taken down to be weighed at The Lion coach office, the cord broke and they fell to the floor. When the startled staff looked down there was a dead man's head.

As a crowd gathered, the coach office owner ordered the boxes to be taken to the Guild Hall where the body of an elderly thin man was found in one box and the body of an elderly thin woman in another.

A surgeon was called who confirmed that the two had died of natural causes and a jury later agreed with him.

It is believed that the boxes were allowed to continue to London for dissection.

But as *The Salopian Journal* commented: 'In the present incidence no blame can be attached to the coach proprietors for conveying such luggage as there was not the slightest smell, nor from the appearance of the boxes, could anyone have supposed that they contained such articles as were found on them.'

The paper concluded: 'We trust the parties will think it is necessary, for the sake of decency, to pack their treasures a little more carefully.'

6

END OF THE ROAD FOR STAGECOACHES AS THE TRAIN ARRIVES

THE EARLY PART OF THE 19TH CENTURY was a golden age for Shrewsbury, as the number of stagecoaches increased with names such as the Stag, the Dart, the Rocket, the Original Salopian, the Young Prince, the Pickwick, the Nimrod and even the strangely titled The Bang-up.

However, due to the furious competitiveness between rival stagecoaches it meant that travelling on them was rarely quiet.

The author Thomas de Quincey wrote:

Once I remember being on top of the Holyhead mail between Shrewsbury and Oswestry, when a tawdry thing from Birmingham, some Tally-ho or High-flyer, all flaunting with green or gold, came up alongside all of us.

What a contrast with our royal simplicity of form and colour in this plebeian wretch.

The single ornament on our dark background of chocolate colour was the mighty shield of the Imperial arms, but emblazoned in proportion as modest as a signet ring bears to a seal of office. Even this was displayed on only a single panel, whispering rather than proclaiming our relations to the mighty State; whilst the Beast from Birmingham, our green and gold friend from false, fleeting perjured Brummagem, had as much writing and painting on its sprawling flanks as would have puzzled a decipherer from the tombs of Luxor.'

He continued: 'The coachman slipped our Royal horses like cheetahs, or hunting leopards, after the affrighted game.

'Passing them without an effort with so lengthening an interval between us as proved in itself the bitterest mockery of their presumption whilst our guard blew back a shattering blast of triumph that was really too painfully full of derision.'

Shrewsbury also enjoyed celebrating its importance as a centre for stagecoaches.

The *Chronicle* reported that on Tuesday, May 28, 1833, the official birthday of King William IV was celebrated in Shrewsbury 'by a novel and interesting spectacle' as eleven coaches belonging to The Lion processed through the streets, drawn by fine horses, driven by men who had 'deservedly gained high characters on the road'.

Afterwards 77 men dined at the Hen & Chickens, Dogpole, which served as a 'tap' to The Lion where coach proprietor Isaac Taylor expressed his joy at being able to contribute to the comfort of the public and the happiness of those he employed.

Every year after that the coaching firms celebrated their success on the King's birthday by parading their carriages through 'the town bedecked with garlands and laurels accompanied by musicians'.

In 1835, Sam Hayward driving the Wonder diverted up Howard Street to witness the laying of the foundation stone for the new Butter Market.

Then in 1836, 15 coaches and two bands paraded through the crowded streets and were the first to pass by the Abbey over the new road, which was being built as part of the improvement of the Holyhead Road. Afterwards, they retired to have dinner at The Lion.

That was the last procession as the King died the following year and by 1838 the railways were beginning to expand all over the country, even though the first trains did not reach Shrewsbury until 1848.

The stagecoaches could not compete with the new transport which provided a cheaper, faster and more comfortable journey.

The extremely bad winter of 1836/37 focused everyone's attention on the coaches' disadvantages. There were exceptionally heavy snowdrifts on the evening of Christmas Day that year and by December 27, 14 mail coaches were abandoned throughout the country and the effect was beginning to tell on Shrewsbury.

A Shropshire resident referred to the town before 1837 as 'a little metropolis to which resorted all the county families for public functions of all kind' but 'the advent of the railway killed all this gay provincial life'.

And another wrote to a friend in Halifax in January 1838: 'Shrewsbury seems to be a declining town. There is very little Sociality left . . . The Manchester and Liverpool Railway to Birmingham has had a very great and disadvantageous effect upon this town, which has almost ceased to be a thoroughfare and it was a great one; consequently many of the coaches have been given up.'

This even caused the population of Shrewsbury to fall, as people moved to find work after cutbacks in the coaching industry.

By 1841, there were 18,285 people in Shrewsbury compared to 21,297 in 1831.

However, Shrewsbury and the owner of The Lion, Isaac Taylor, did not give up without a fight. On one unforgettable occasion in 1838, the Shrewsbury Wonder left London at the same time as the train for Birmingham, and actually arrived in the Midlands city first.

When the Hon. Thomas Kenyon, of Pradoe, Shropshire, a famous whip, amateur coachman and Holyhead Road Commissioner, was rewarded with a commemorative plate at a dinner in Shrewsbury in 1842, a toast was drunk proposing 'confusion to the rail-roads and a high gallows and a windy day to all enemies of the whip'.

While rivals gave up, Taylor used his entrepreneurial skills to keep The Lion as a coaching centre for 25 years after the railways first appeared.

He took on the trains by putting up a sign in the inn announcing that fares on the Shrewsbury Wonder were being reduced. He said that when the coach reached Birmingham, passengers could choose either to stay on the Wonder or catch the train for the second part of their journey.

When the Shrewsbury & Chester line opened in 1848 Taylor operated a bus between the station and The Lion, even providing accommodation for passengers who arrived on the London train at 2.10am. They were taken to the hotel to await the departure of the Aberystwyth mail coach at 4am.

In 1849, the Shrewsbury Railway Station offered five-hour train journeys to London and the number of stagecoaches soon dropped to only six as the mail was switched on to the railways. Taylor responded by taking over the valuable agency to distribute those parcels.

The end of the road for the golden age of coaching came in July 1861 when the *Chronicle* announced: '27th July. Sale at The Lion, property of Mr George Curtis, 30 first-class coach or post horses, now engaged in working the Shrewsbury and Aberystwyth Mail and Coaches and well-known on the road for their fast pace and powers of endurance. Will be sold without reserve in consequence of the opening of a portion of the Welsh railway, and the retirement of Mr Curtis from working the Aberystwyth coaches.'

It was the end of an era, but their memory still lives on as some of today's Shrewsbury's Park and Ride buses are named after the town's stagecoaches.

7

HAVING A BALL IN THE BALLROOM

QUEEN ANNE, WHO ASCENDED THE THRONE on March 8, 1702, first made the Social Season fashionable and later on in the 18th century Shrewsbury had its own season.

There was horse racing, firstly at Kingsland and later at Bicton Heath, in September; regular theatre plays, concerts, walks, rides, bowls, tennis and an occasional Flower Show plus tea-drinking parties which had become fashionable.

But the event of the year was the annual Shrewsbury Hunt in the autumn with its Hunt Ball, which lawyer John Ashby had seized from the Raven and moved to the newly-furnished, luxuriously decorated, gilt mirrored Assembly Room – or Ballroom – which was now the social centre for the county set.

A fascinating glimpse into society life at the end of the 18th century in Shrewsbury with its hunt ball and dinners is given in a letter, reported in *Shropshire Notes and Queries*, that an Irish boy, boarding at Shrewsbury School, wrote to his mother on December 27, 1787.

After telling her how he had dined with his aunt in Shrewsbury on Christmas Day he continued:

> I saw the Earl of Portarlington on Monday with his lady go from The Lion in their own coach, which was so heavy that four horses were scarcely able to stir out of The Lion yard. But yesterday I saw more than this; it was Miss Pultney's birthday, and she was of age yesterday, so there was great rejoicings. The British ensign was displayed from the mount before the Castle, where he lives, and the Jack from the top of the Castle, a flag was displayed from the battlement of St Mary's tower.
>
> An ox was roasted whole in the meadow behind our house, a sheep in the Raven street, and another before the Town Hall (Papa knows all these places) and as much drink (strong beer) given out from the Castle as they asked for, which (were) open for anyone to drink what they pleased, with flags displayed from the tops of them. At night the Raven Street and mount at the Castle were illuminated and some houses here and there in other parts of the town.

Mr Pultney also gave a ball and supper at The Lion to which he gave a general invitation in the newspaper. I got to the door of the Assembly Room just in time to see Mr and Miss P get out of their coach. He looked very well last night and like a gentleman. I saw her for the first time; she is not very handsome, but I think she is a pretty-looking girl; she was dressed in a kind of a chocolate-coloured satin, trimmed with ermine, she seemed to me to have no hoop.

They say she is to have £16,000 a year in her own possession now that she is at age.

Last week (was) the hunt week, too, when there were fine dinners at The Lion every day, a concert on Tuesday evening, and a ball on Thursday, when I went also to the door of the Assembly Room to see the company go in, unknown to Mr J, but Mrs J gave us leave.

Well, I have told you enough of all this I believe.

He then sends various messages to different members of the family and signs off L.L.B.

 ☐   ☐   ☐

One of the most famous guests to visit the ballroom was Prince William of Gloucester, who later became King William IV (1830-37). He stayed at the hotel and attended a ball here in 1803. However, there is no record of whether he brought the Irish actress, Dorothea Bland, to Shrewsbury whom he had been living with since 1791 and who had borne him ten illegitimate children during their 20-year relationship.

A year earlier, another unusual guest ended up sleeping in the Assembly Room or Ballroom because major repairs were being carried out to the hotel.

Author Thomas De Quincey (1785-1859) came to The Lion as a 17-year-old in 1802 on his way to catch the early mail train to London. He arrived at the hotel reception two hours after nightfall after walking to Shrewsbury from Oswestry and, as he had already booked and there was no bed for him, he was put up in the Ballroom.

In *Confessions of an English Opium-Eater* he said:

I stepped into the sumptuous room allotted to me. It was a ballroom of noble proportions – lighted, if I chose to issue orders, by three gorgeous chandeliers, not loosely wrapped up in paper, but sparkling through all their thickets of crystal branches, and flashing back the soft rays of my tall waxen lights.

Long before midnight the household (with the exception of a solitary waiter) had retired to rest.

Suddenly, I heard a sound of wheels, which, however, soon died off into some remote quarter. I guessed at the truth, that it was the Holyhead Mail wheeling off on its primary duty of delivering its bags at the post office. In a few minutes it was announced as having changed horses; and I was off to London.

Robert Southey gives a wonderful description of the hustle and bustle at a coaching inn, such as The Lion, which De Quincey experienced in his *Letter from England*. He writes:

The perpetual stir and bustle of the inn is as surprising as it is wearisome. Doors opening and shutting, bells ringing, voices calling to the waiter from every quarter, while he cries 'coming' to one room and hurries away to another. Everybody is in a hurry here; either they are going off in packets, and are hastening their preparations to embark; or they have just arrived, and are impatient to be on the road homeward. Every now-and-then a carriage rattles up to the door with a rapidity which makes the very house shake. The man who cleans the boots is running in one direction, the barber with his powder-bag in another; here goes the barber's boy with his hot water and razors; there comes the clean linen from the washer-woman; and the hall is full of porters and sailors bringing in luggage, or bearing it away; now you hear a horn blow because the post is coming in, and in the middle of the night you are awakened by another because it is going out. Nothing is done in England without noise, and yet noise is the only thing they forget in the bill.

☐ ☐ ☐

The 18th century Assembly Room, or Ballroom, which architect experts John Newman and Nikolaus Pevsner describe as 'a wonderfully complete example of mid-Georgian suite of rooms for public entertainment,' has hardly changed over the centuries.

Visitors today can still see the same delicate colouring on the walls and the emblematic figures of Music and Dancing painted on the door panels, the two music galleries, the chandeliers and the moulded plaster decorations in the Robert Adam style. They can imagine what it must have been like when the famous Signor Niccolo Paganini gave a concert here in 1833.

Tucked away at the bottom of page three of the August 9, 1833, edition of the

Shrewsbury Chronicle edition was an advertisement for the Paganini concert. It said:

> Under distinguished patronage, Signor Paganini respectfully announces to the Nobility and Gentry of Shrewsbury that he will give a Grand Vocal and Instrumental Concert at The Lion Ballroom on Thursday evening, August the 15th being positively the only time he can possibly have the honour of appearing before them previous to his departure for the Court of St Petersburg on which occasion he has engaged those highly celebrated Vocalists, Miss Wells and Miss Watson, likewise Mr Watson, composer to the Theatres Royal, English Opera House and Covent Gardens, and member of the Royal Academy of Music who will preside at the Piano Forte. Tickets 2/6d each (12.5p today) may be had at Mr Eddoes, Corn Market, Shrewsbury. The concert will commence precisely at 8 o' clock.

As can be seen from the advertisement, of which a framed copy of the original programme is still on display in the hotel foyer, long sentences were preferred in the first part of the 19th century.

To get Niccolo Paganini, a 19th century equivalent to a rock star today, must have been an incredible achievement for Shrewsbury. The musician, born in Genoa, Italy, on October 27, 1782, had dramatically changed the writing of violin music, astounding audiences with techniques that included harmonies and near impossible fingerings and bowings. His Caprice No. 24 in A Minor, Op. 1, is among his best compositions, a work that has inspired many top composers.

As a former editor of the *Shrewsbury Chronicle,* I eagerly turned to the August 16, 1833, edition of the paper to see how their equivalent to the arts critic treated this amazing concert coup for the town.

The first time I looked through the paper I missed it. But on the second time of searching I found what I thought was the beginning of the review at the bottom of page three.

Without a headline it said: 'Paganini Concert at The Lion Rooms, last night, was crowded, not only by the first families in the county, but by many from Montgomeryshire and other parts of the Principality.'

I immediately scanned up to the top of the page for the continuation of the story. But there was nothing. I was speechless, but I wouldn't have been if I had been the paper's editor in 1833 when the reporter arrived in the office the next morning after obviously burning the midnight oil to produce that paragraph.

Incidentally, the Shrewsbury Summer Season re-enacted the Paganini concert on Friday, August 15, 2008, at The Lion to celebrate the 175th anniversary of the event. Organised by Maggie Love, the then Arts Development Officer at Shrewsbury and Atcham Borough Council, the concert attracted a sell-out audience as violin virtuoso Madeleine Easton, helped by musicians Claire Surman and Gary Cooper, played the exact violin pieces performed by Paganini in 1833.

In December 1990, the hotel spent £50,000 on restoring the Ballroom to its former glory. The owners worked with English Heritage to return the room to its original colour scheme trying 52 paint samples as they had uncovered 15 layers of paint, which had been applied over the centuries.

At a guest lunch at the hotel to re-open the newly-restored Ballroom the then Mayor of Shrewsbury, Councillor Mrs Jane Coward, recalled attending dances there in her younger years and sitting on the edge of the room waiting to be asked for a dance.

'We hope to enjoy these wonderful surroundings which you have provided for the people of Shrewsbury and Atcham,' she told the manager, Matthew Salomonson, and the then hotel owners, Trust House Forte group.

However, it wasn't just concerts that were held in the Ballroom. In 1822 and 1830, Madame Tussauds brought their famous life-size wax models of celebrities to Shrewsbury on a national tour.

In an advertisement they proclaimed, by the permission of the Right Worshipful Mayor of Shrewsbury: 'Madame Tussauds and Sons have the honour most respectfully to inform the ladies and gentlemen of Shrewsbury and its Vicinity that their Splendid Exhibition, which has been considerably enlarged since their most successful visit in 1822, will be opened for a short season in the Great Assembly Room, The Lion Inn, in a few days of which due notice will be given. Admittance one shilling (5p).'

The notice added that Madame Tussauds had 'redressed their figures in splendid costumes and also added a great number of new and interesting characters, from the high and elevated, to the most infamous and diabolical, among which latter class will be found the likeness of Burke and Hare, which have been viewed by 60,000 persons.'

Irish immigrants Brendan 'Dynes' Burke and William Hare were serial murderers in the 1820s who had sold the corpses of 17 of their victims to Dr Robert Knox, a private anatomy lecturer whose students were drawn from Edinburgh Medical College, to provide bodies for dissection. They included Burke's mistress, Helen McDougal, and Hare's wife, Margaret Laird.

☐ ☐ ☐

Meanwhile, singer Jenny Lind, who is reported in many booklets and articles to have given two concerts at the Ballroom, actually sang instead at the Music Hall on both occasions in 1849 and 1856.

This was because in the early 19th century a larger place than The Lion was needed to put on plays and concerts. Edward Haycock, the grandson of William Haycock who rebuilt The Lion in the late 1770s, designed the Music Hall in the Square, which was opened in 1840.

Born Johanna Maria Lind in Sweden on October 6, 1820, Jenny, who was known as the Swedish Nightingale, was one of the most highly regarded soprano singers of the 19th century performing worldwide.

It was thanks to the local Choral Society who invited the 'Queen of Song' to Shrewsbury for a concert on Monday, February 26, 1849, and it is believed she stayed at The Lion Hotel on the Sunday and Monday nights.

Her visit certainly captured people's imagination with crowds outside the theatre and a full house inside.

The *Eddowes Journal*, later the *Salopian Journal*, which was a Tory supporting paper, reported in its Wednesday, February 28 edition: 'The glut of carriages in the evening, from seven to eight o' clock, and the concourse of people to witness her arrival and departure were such as have not been witnessed in Shrewsbury for some years; crowds occupied all the adjacent streets and passages during the entire evening in order to catch the most distant sounds of the lady's warblings.'

The paper went on: 'There was not a vacant seat, or standing place, in the entire, spacious Music Hall; the orchestra was a rising semi amphitheatre of heads and several gentlemen of great respectability were forced to put up with an orchestral seat.'

The story also brought out the competitive dog eats dog world of newspapers, even in the 19th century.

The town rival to the *Eddowes Journal*, the Liberal supporting *Shrewsbury Chronicle*, which came out on Friday, March 2, said rather sniffily in its first paragraph: 'The charming Jenny Lind, whose fame as the first vocalist of the day is equalled by the still more ennobling halo that attaches to her name in the cause of charity and benevolence, gave a concert on Monday evening.'

Ironically, the event, also starring Miss Kenneth, Signor Belletti, Mr G A Seymour on the violin, Mr Hiles on the organ and pianist and conductor M. Benedict, raised just under £800 for charity.

The *Eddowes Journal* hit back at the *Chronicle* in its March 7 edition saying:

'Our contemporary of Friday had a fair opportunity on being facetious on the subject as well as dilating on the shades of flexibility in the lady's voice and revelling in all the luxuriant verbiage of the dilettanti.'

Stung by the criticism, the *Chronicle* in its March 9 edition retorted: 'Our contemporary of Wednesday had wasted a good deal of fine writing on a song that was not sung at all.'

The *Eddowes Journal* had said of the concert: 'The Cavatina, Deh Vieni Non Tardar, (Come don't delay) was brilliantly and beautifully given out and gave an exercise at once to the commanding range of her voice, in all its bell-like singleness and splendour of tone.'

However, as the *Chronicle* pointed out. 'Mademoiselle Lind did not sing the Cavatina; she substituted it by request for Casta Diva.'

The *Eddowes Journal* wasn't finished. Like many a journalist down the ages, if there is a mistake in the paper, the easiest people to blame are the printers.

In the next edition they explained: 'A trifling error occurred in our notice of Mademoiselle Lind's performance, for the usual practice of referring the compositor to the printed programme for taking up the leading passages of the songs in which Casta Diva was given in place of the piece substituted, printers not being necessarily familiar with the language that breathes of the sweet south, and comes like kisses from a lady's mouth.'

In between her first and second concerts in Shrewsbury, Jenny Lind married Otto Goldschmidt in 1852 when she was 31.

Her second town concert, again at the Music Hall, was on Monday, May 5, 1856. This time Jenny Lind Goldschmidt was assisted by her husband on the piano; Herr Ernst on violin, Signor Piatti on violin cello and Mr W H Weiss.

Jenny was still as popular as ever with her Shrewsbury audience and special trains were put on for the concert from as far away as Wolverhampton calling at Shifnal, Oakengates, Wellington, Walcot and Upton Magna, plus one from Oswestry and another from Ludlow, with them all returning at 10.45pm.

However, she didn't quite get the same glowing reviews in the local press.

The *Eddowes Journal* said of the star: 'Since we saw her last, she seems to have aged considerably.' And it added: 'We will venture an opinion, that in the lower register of her voice, she lacks some trifle of that clear and bell-like tone which characterised it in times gone by. Having dared to say thus much, we are bound also to say, that in our opinion, there is no living singer that can claim an audience like Jenny Lind. At the conclusion she was greeted with most rapturous applause, amidst which she retired.'

8

GREAT EXPECTATIONS OF CHARLES DICKENS AT THE LION

PROBABLY THE MOST FAMOUS COMMENT about The Lion Hotel was by the novelist Charles Dickens who stayed there on August 12, 1858, with his friend and illustrator, Hablot K Browne, otherwise know as Phiz.

They were given rooms in what was then an annexe and Dickens wrote to one of his daughters: 'We have the strangest little rooms, the ceilings of which I can touch with my hand. The windows bulge out over the street as if they were little stern windows of a ship. And a door opens out of the sitting room on to a little open gallery with plants in it where one leans over a queer old rail.'

It wasn't the only time that Dickens stayed at The Lion. It appears he enjoyed the quirky hotel, where visitors even today can see the Dickens room complete with plaque.

However, one writer, who was not so impressed with the hotel, was the America novelist and short story writer Nathaniel Hawthorne (1804-1864).

Nathaniel, who was rewarded for writing the presidential election campaign biography for his friend Franklin Pierce by being appointed the U.S. Consular in Liverpool, came to Shrewsbury with his wife Sophia and three children in 1855 and stayed at The Lion. He wrote: 'It is an uncheerful old hotel, which takes upon itself to be in the best class of English country hotel, and charges the best price; very dark in the lower apartments, pervaded with a musty odour but provided with a white-neck-clothed waiter, who spares no ceremony in serving the joints of mutton.'

Dickens had stayed at The Lion 20 years previously when he records in his 1838 Journal that on Wednesday, October 31 he and his wife Catherine had attended the Shrewsbury Theatre to see *A Roland for an Oliver* before leaving the next day to travel on to Llangollen.

The author is known to have visited Shrewsbury on a number of other occasions, including May 10, 1852, when he appeared at the Music Hall in the comedy *Not so bad as we seem* or *Many sides to a character*, which was written by Sir Edward Bulwer-Lytton. The performance concluded with an original farce in one act by Charles Dickens and Mark Lemon entitled *Mr Nightingale's Diary*.

It is probable that Dickens stayed at The Lion more than twice, with some saying he wrote Pickwick Papers here. When he booked in at the hotel he had two rooms, a bedroom upstairs and a lounge below complete with desk.

Charles John Huffam Dickens, who was born on February 7, 1812, in Portsmouth, moved to London when he was three. His first job was at Warrens Blacking Warehouse where he was pasting labels on shoe polish. When he was 15 he joined the law office of Ellis and Blackmore, attorneys, of Holborn Court, Gray's Inn, as a junior clerk, before becoming a freelance journalist concentrating on court and later political reporting plus some writing. His first stories were serialised in magazines, and rather than wait until he had finished the whole story, Dickens often wrote the episodes week by week.

He learnt to leave the end of each part on a cliffhanger so the public would look forward to the next instalment. His first novel, the *Pickwick Papers*, was completed this way in March 1836.

A month later, Dickens married Catherine Tomson Hogarth (1816-1879), the daughter of George Hogarth, editor of the *Evening Chronicle,* and they went on to have ten children.

He continued to be a prolific writer and became the most popular English novelist of the Victorian era producing classics of English literature and the most iconic characters as he showed his concern for social reform.

In the summer of 1858, Dickens separated from his wife, although divorce would have been unthinkable for a man so well known.

That same year, Dickens had been approached for help by the Great Ormond Street Hospital which was suffering a major financial crisis. On February 9, he spoke at the hospital's first annual festival dinner at Freemasons' Hall and later gave a public reading of *A Christmas Carol* at St Martin-in-the-Fields church hall. The events were such a success that the hospital raised enough funds to buy the neighbouring house, No. 48 Great Ormond Street, and increase their bed capacity from 20 to 75.

This gave Dickens the idea of earning money by giving public readings of his work. He began with *A Christmas Carol* in London and then set off on an ambitious and gruelling tour through England, Scotland and Ireland beginning with a performance in Clifton on August 2 and finishing in Brighton three months later on November 13. Altogether, he gave 87 performances, on some days giving both a matinée and an evening show, including one at the Shrewsbury Music Hall on August 13, 1858, when he stayed at The Lion and wrote his views on the hotel to one of his daughters.

The *Shrewsbury Chronicle* had obviously learnt the importance of reviews giving Dickens much more editorial space than Paganini 25 years previously.

However, news sense seemed to be lacking a little on the paper as the visit of the most famous novelist in the country at that time could make it only to the bottom of page four – and that was underneath the births, marriages and deaths notices.

The reporter wrote:

> We were pleased last night to observe an audience – intelligent to know they would be – assembled to hear this most popular of English authors read *A Christmas Carol*, one of his own inimitable stories.
>
> There are few, indeed, in most classes of English Society, who have not been delighted with the writings of Dickens; and however people may cavil at his taste in thus reading his own works, the sight of so successful a writer is a treat of so rich a character that we are inclined to accept the good without a murmur.
>
> We shall not enter into a detailed notice of Mr Dickens' reading last night, much as we would have been pleased to refer to some of the many happy hits he made.
>
> Notwithstanding the wretched place, in which our Music Hall undoubtedly is, Mr Dickens' reading was so effective that his audience wept with him over the pathetic history of Tiny Tim and laughed as heartily over many of the highly humorous scenes in this enchanting story.
>
> The characters in the book all became real and living under the author's treatment – for our readers need not to be told that Mr Dickens' dramatic powers are of the highest order of excellence.
>
> On the whole the audience were delighted, as was also Mr Dickens we should imagine, by the cordial and even enthusiastic reception he met with in Shrewsbury.

Shropshire was obviously one of his favourite places.

In *A Tale of Two Cities* one of the characters mentioned is Sydney Carton of old Shrewsbury School while Mr Stryver, Darnay's defence lawyer, has a portrait of 'Hanging' Judge Jeffreys, who was from Wem, on his office wall.

In addition, it is believed Miss Havisham in *Great Expectations* is based on a wealthy recluse, Elizabeth Parker, whom Dickens met while staying in Newport, Shropshire, at the aptly named Havisham Court.

And after visiting Tong, Dickens used it as the final resting place for Little Nell and her Grandfather in *The Old Curiosity Shop*.

☐   ☐   ☐

Interestingly, when a £5m film of *A Christmas Carol* was made in March and April 1984 Shrewsbury was chosen as the setting.

It starred George C Scott, Frank Finlay, Susannah York and Edward Woodward, plus six-year-old Tony Walters, of Plaish Park Farm, near Church Stretton, as Tiny Tim, and 450 people from the town as extras.

The 100-minute film is considered by many to be the best version of Dickens' ghost classic, which had a world premiere before the Queen at London's Classic Haymarket and a gala charity premiere in Shrewsbury followed by a week-long run at the town's Empire Cinema in December 1984.

Although the town was turned into Victorian London with the help of 75 tons of salt and 400 gallons of foam, many of centre buildings are easily recognisable, including the Market Hall in The Square, the Parade Shopping Centre and Tanner's wine shop.

Writing in the *Chronicle* about the filming, hotel manager Matthew Salomonson said of the film crew's visit:

> The Lion has never seen an invasion quite like it! The influx of 50 additional guests demanded the bar stayed open into the early hours of the morning, yet without exception they wanted breakfast at 6am.
>
> To say these casually dressed people were totally different to the traditional type of clientele would be an understatement, but they left a lasting impression on the hotel and staff during their eight-week stay.
>
> So much so that the hotel felt positively eerie for quite a while after the film crew left Shrewsbury.
>
> The daily routine and lifestyle of the hotel were turned upside down the day the 'film army' hit Shrewsbury. For the first few days of the invasion all staff were placed under intense pressure.
>
> Then there was the colossal amount of laundry. Not only from the film crew resident at the hotel, but all those connected with the production, processed their laundry through the hotel.
>
> When we first had an inkling that there were people reconnoitering for a film location in Shrewsbury we did not realise the immense scale of the operation. The enormity of the task was driven home to us when they ordered some basic supplies for shooting, which included several hundred toilet rolls and nearly 100 light bulbs!
>
> Right from the outset our staff seemed to get along very well with the crew and they were prepared to put in a lot of hard, extra work to adjust to their needs. The staff were put under a tremendous amount of strain, but they were understanding and helpful – a credit to the hotel and to the industry.

He added: 'The Lion Hotel always welcomes children of all ages, but our facilities were certainly put to the test during the auditions for *A Christmas Carol*. It seemed that for several days the lounges were invaded by thousands of children and their doting mothers, but not being Scrooges the staff seemed to take it all in their stride.'

One of those town extras was Martin Wood, Shrewsbury's Town Crier, who was Edward Woodward's stand-in and the double for Michael Carter, who played the Spirit of Christmas Future.

Martin, who as an official town guide still does *A Christmas Carol* tours more than 25 years later, said it was a magical time for Shrewsbury and a memorable six weeks for the local people who took part.

After filming, the props were all taken away – apart from one that was left behind.

Scrooge had premonitions of the 'tombstone' of Ebenezer Scrooge and the gravestone is still in the churchyard of St Chad's today.

Interestingly, Gerald Dickens, the great, great grandson of Charles Dickens, puts on one-man shows of the author's works including *A Christmas Carol; Mr Dickens is Coming; Nicholas Nickleby* and *Sketches by Boz*, and regularly performs in theatres, art and literary festivals as well as hotels, stately homes and cruise ships.

He will be coming to The Lion in February 2012, the 200th anniversary of his great, great grandfather's birth, to give one of his shows.

9

THE LION HOTEL, ORIGIN OF CHARLES DARWIN'S EPIC ADVENTURE

For most travellers, The Lion is the end of their journey as they arrive in Shrewsbury for a short break to explore this historic town.

However, for one intrepid traveller The Lion was the start of an epic adventure.

Twenty-two-year-old Charles Darwin departed the hotel in haste on Monday, September 5, 1831, by stagecoach to London on his way to join HMS Beagle for a five-year trip, which would end with him writing his controversial book on evolution, *The Origin of Species*.

The reason Darwin left the town in such a rush was that a second person had been offered the job as naturalist on the ship, which was due to set sail later that month, and the young Shrewsbury scientist feared he might miss his opportunity.

Darwin had been offered the position a week earlier for what had planned to be a two-year survey of South America and he had accepted it. However, his father, Robert, supported by Charles' sisters, refused to let him go saying the trip would get in the way of him becoming a clergyman.

After what must have been a heated family discussion his father relented and said he could go, if he could find a man with common sense who thought it would be a good idea.

Darwin wrote to his Cambridge professor of botany, the Rev John Stevens Henslow, while his father wrote to his brother Josiah Wedgwood II. The next afternoon Charles rode over to his uncle's home at Maer Hall, just over the border in Staffordshire, near Market Drayton and Newcastle-under-Lyme, for the start of the hunting season and to put his case to the member of the famous Wedgwood pottery family.

The plan worked. His uncle wrote to Darwin's father answering all the objections and Robert agreed to support his son financially.

Since the Whitehall Admiralty hadn't heard from Darwin for a few days, they presumed he had changed his mind and offered the job to someone else.

Darwin hurried down to London on the first available stagecoach to see

The Dickens bedroom. Where Charles Dickens stayed in August 1858 and where guests can rest today. Notice the windows, which Dickens said 'bulge out over the street as if they were little stern windows of a ship'. [Pictures on this page: Richard Bishop]

The Dickens suite. Dickens is believed to have used this room, which was connected to the bedroom above by an internal staircase, as a lounge and writing room.

The Dickens balcony. A close-up of the balcony which Dickens described as having 'a queer old rail'.

The Ballroom or The Assembly Room built in the late 1770s has changed little over the centuries. Architect experts John Newman and Nikolaus Pevsner describe it as 'an amazing room, of priceless value to the student and lover of art'.
[Pictures on this page: Richard Bishop]

The Dining Room below the Ballroom.

The Lion Hotel dominates the top of Wyle Cop today. [Pictures on this page: Richard Bishop]

Darwin cartoon. Every year since 2003, the town has hosted the Shrewsbury International Cartoon Festival, which has attracted around 40 full-time, professional cartoonists and caricaturists from the UK and abroad, including Australia and Canada, all of whom stay at The Lion. Hotel owner Howard Astbury commissioned one of them, Bill Stott, to draw this Darwin cartoon which hangs in reception.

A drawing of the Shrewsbury Wonder stagecoach which is inside St Julian's Church.

The impressive tapestry lounge at The Lion. [Picture: Richard Bishop]

Friday 15th August
PAGANINI
at the LION

Madeleine Easton – *violin*
Claire Sermans – *soprano*
Gary Cooper – *piano*

This evening celebrates 175 years since Paganini played in the Adam Ballroom at the Lion Hotel Shrewsbury

The evening will include the exact violin pieces performed by **Paganini** and arias from the original evening in August 15th 1833. There will be music recreating the event by the violinist ***Madeleine Easton***. She will perform a selection of the renowned Caprices during the meal and then perform with ***Gary Cooper*** and ***Claire Sermans*** in the wonderful Adam Ballroom.

It will be a remarkable evening of culinary and musical enjoyment and a wonderful chance to recreate and celebrate the visit to Shrewsbury of one of musical history's most remarkable figures.

Tickets from the Music Hall
Box Office – 01743 281281

Dinner And Concert £40
Concert Only £15

HATCHERS
solicitors

To celebrate the 175th anniversary of Signor Niccolo Paganini's concert at The Lion, the Shrewsbury Summer Season re-enacted it on Friday, August 15, 2008.

The Hayward Restaurant was given a facelift in February 2011, at the same time as award-winning Michelin chef Ian Matfin came to work at the hotel.
[Picture: Richard Bishop]

Captain Robert FitzRoy who asked him if he was still interested in the position, as the other person had turned it down. Charles again accepted the job, and was told to report to Plymouth for the new sailing date of October 10, although the ship didn't eventually leave until 11am on Tuesday, December 27.

On board the Beagle, his new home and base for the next five years was the chart room which, after allowing for the bookshelves, cabinets, an oven and a washstand, was just 6ft by 8ft with 5ft of headroom. To make matters worse the mizzenmast came up through the floor and there was a large 4ft by 6ft chart table in the middle of the room.

The first home for Charles Robert Darwin was The Mount where he had been born on February 12, 1809, to his father Robert and mother, Susannah, who died when her son was only eight.

When he was nine, he joined his brother, Erasmus, at Shrewsbury Grammar School (now the town library). However, seven years later, on June 17, 1825, his father took him out of the school for idleness, telling him: 'You care for nothing but shooting, dogs and rat catching and will be a disgrace to yourself and all your family.'

The young Darwin didn't enjoy life at the austere Shrewsbury School where only foot pans were available for washing and 20-30 boys shared a dormitory which had a single window, damp beds and poor food. Neither did he rate the curriculum of mainly classics, thinking it was a waste of time.

He preferred to roam around the River Severn, observing beetles, spiders, fish and frogs and conducting experiments in the tool shed at the bottom of his garden, which he and his brother had turned into a laboratory.

As Robert, and his father before him, had studied medicine, Erasmus and Charles were sent to the University of Edinburgh to continue the family tradition. But Charles found the subject boring and not helped by his fear of blood.

However, there he met John Edmondstone, a freed black slave from Guyana, who inspired him with tales about the South American tropical rain forests and taught him taxidermy, the skill of stuffing animals, which would prove extremely useful to Darwin on HMS Beagle.

In April 1827, Darwin quit medical school and his father arranged for him to go to Christ's College, Cambridge University, to become a clergyman. But he didn't take his studies seriously, preferring to attend the Rev Henslow's botany lectures.

Still, in January 1831, he managed to pass all his final exams and finished 10th out of the 178 who graduated.

Darwin began looking for a rural parish where he could be a clergyman and continue his rural studies.

Later that year, he returned to Shrewsbury where he joined Professor Sedgwick for a summer geology expedition to Wales and became addicted to the subject. He applied to be a naturalist on HMS Beagle, and when he returned from Wales to his home in Shrewsbury, there was a letter waiting offering him the job.

When he did eventually join the ship and crew of 73, Darwin was immediately seasick as he left Plymouth Sound, a problem that dogged him throughout his trip.

As the ship called at the Canary Islands, the Cape Verde Islands, Brazil, Tierra del Fuego, and the Falkland Islands, Darwin became engrossed in the job, sending many specimens of animals, fossils and plants back to his Cambridge professor for further analysis.

Life was so hectic that by the time he arrived in Montevideo, Uruguay, he sent a letter home asking his father if he could hire a servant on £60 a year to help him. He agreed and Charles employed the Beagle's odd job man, Syms Corvington, as his servant.

Eventually, the HMS Beagle reached the Galapagos Islands on September 16, 1835, the scene of Darwin's major research on his evolution theory. He then travelled on to Tahiti, New Zealand, Australia and South Africa before returning up the Atlantic, docking at Falmouth on October 2, 1836.

The journey, which was due to last two years, in fact, took four years, nine months and five days, of which 18 months had been spent at sea and three years three months on land.

Darwin immediately set off from Cornwall to Shrewsbury by stagecoach, and as he arrived so late in the evening, it is believed he spent the night at The Lion before arriving at his home for breakfast to a surprised but delighted family.

Early in the following year, Darwin moved into 36 Great Marlborough Street, London, where he continued to write up his research still helped by his servant, Syms.

However, he continued to return to Shrewsbury, keeping in touch particularly with his cousin, Emma Wedgwood of Maer Hall, whom he married on January 29, 1839. The couple had ten children, three of whom died young.

He carried on his work, writing at the time: 'I do not remember any mental pursuits excepting those of collecting stones, etc., gardening, and about this time often going with my father in his carriage, telling him of my lessons, and seeing game and other wild birds, which was a great delight to me. I was born a naturalist.'

But his poor health forced the family to move from London to Downs House in the hamlet of Downe, Kent, in 1842.

His illness became worse and it was so bad that he could not attend his father's funeral at Shrewsbury in November 1848.

The Mount stayed as the family home for another 18 years before it was sold and is today occupied by the District Valuer and Valuation Officer of Shrewsbury.

Darwin continued his work being awarded the Royal Medal by the Royal Society in 1853, and on November 22, 1859 published his work entitled *On the Origin of Species by means of Natural Selection*, priced at 15 shillings (75p). There were 1,250 copies printed, most of which were sold on the first day.

His controversial views caused an outcry then and the debate has been going on ever since.

When a gale blew down the top 50ft of St Mary's Church spire on Sunday, February 11, 1894, the day before the anniversary of Darwin's birth, and while the council were debating putting up a controversial statue of Darwin in the town, the vicar said it was divine retribution.

Scaffolding, which had been put up by workmen who were due to return to work on the Monday, crashed down, along with part of the spire into the nave which had been full with more than 300 worshippers only an hour or so previously.

Preaching in the wrecked sanctuary on the following Sunday, the vicar, the Rev Newdegate Poyntz, told the congregation: 'Could anyone in the future doubt the providence of God? Not one soul was lost. Could they, therefore, doubt that God's hand was present throughout all and that He was guiding and ruling all?'

Referring to the councillors and their debate he continued:

The fall of the spire should stop for ever, in their mouths at least, the jargon about natural laws, natural forces and the like, so common in this present day. One day this month a certain event occurred in Shrewsbury and a few days afterwards the spire was blown down by an Act of God. Was there any connection between the two events?

If he was right, it was at least possible many had received a warning. Let them act upon it. If they pondered well over his remarks, and digested them, they ought to bring in during the week, sufficient funds to restore the church twice over.

The sermon caused 14 readers to write letters to the *Chronicle* over the next two weeks, most of them agreeing with the vicar.

The paper in its opinion column tried to be more conciliatory. It said: 'Where so many valuable opinions have been expressed, it is not for us to say who are right, nor are we sufficiently concerned to venture on the assertion that any particular opinion is erroneous.

'What we are anxious about is not the cause of the disaster, but the restoration of the structure. Instead of theory let us have practice. Now is the time, not for talk, but for benevolence.' Funds for the £6,000 repair bill for St Mary's were eventually found and a statue of Charles Darwin, who died on April 19, 1882, and was buried a week later at Westminster Abbey on April 26, was placed outside what is now Shrewsbury Library and can be seen today.

10

MAD JACK - SHREWSBURY'S MOST ECCENTRIC MP

THE MOST ECCENTRIC MP to have used The Lion Hotel as a political base was John 'Mad Jack' Mytton, whose ancestor Thomas Mytton, the Bailiff of Shrewsbury, allowed Henry Tudor to enter Shrewsbury by 'stepping over his belly' as he lay on the Welsh Bridge in 1485.

'Mad Jack' was born on September 30, 1796, to a family of Shropshire squires. His father died when he was two, which meant he inherited the family seat of Halston Hall, near Oswestry, when he was 21. As it was then worth about £60,000, the equivalent to nearly £5m today, with an income of £10,000 a year and equivalent to £716,000 today, there was little incentive for him to work hard.

He was sent to Westminster School where, after one year, he was expelled for fighting a master and then to Harrow where he lasted just three days before he was thrown out. His family decided it was better for him to be educated by a series of private tutors on whom Mad Jack played many practical jokes, including leaving a horse in one of their bedrooms.

Despite his educational record, he was still given a place at Cambridge where he arrived with 2,000 bottles of port to see him through his studies. He found life there boring and left without graduating to go on the Grand Tour around Europe's main capitals before joining the 7th Hussars in France as part of the occupying army following Napoleon's defeat.

But, after much gambling and drinking, he soon resigned his commission and returned home to claim his family inheritance.

In 1819, he decided to continue the family tradition by becoming MP for Shrewsbury and was easily elected – helped no doubt by offering constituents £10 each if they would vote for him and spending £10,000 on bribes.

He celebrated at being elected MP in typical Mad Jack fashion. While he was being carried shoulder high by the enthusiastic burgesses back to The Lion Hotel for a celebratory dinner, he leapt from on high into the hotel bar through the window in a shower of glass. Charles G Harper says in his book *The Holyhead Road*: 'No one was surprised for his was a freakish nature; but they would have been astonished if he had walked in, in the normal way, by the door.'

Mad Jack found the debates boring and attended Parliament only once – and that was for just 30 minutes. He preferred to spend his time hunting, gambling and horse racing with his horse Euphrates winning The Gold Cup in 1825.

A year later, because of a bet, he rode his horse into the Bedford Hotel, Leamington Spa, up the grand staircase, on to the balcony, from where he jumped still on his horse over the startled diners in the restaurant below and out on to the Parade.

Since he was ten he had owned his own pack of hounds and had 150 pairs of hunting breeches, 700 pairs of hand-made hunting boots, 1,000 hats and 3,000 shirts plus 2,000 dogs. His favourite dogs were fed on steak and champagne while his horse, Baronet, had the freedom of the house and would lie in front of the fire with Jack, who would go hunting in all weathers, usually stripping off naked during the chase.

Once when a tough Shropshire miner disturbed his hunt Mad Jack challenged him to a bare-knuckle fight, which lasted 20 rounds – before the miner gave up.

His biographer, Charles Apperley, said that one day Mytton, who was 'somewhat sprung by wine' while drinking in The Lion, was told there was a box in the coach office for him, containing two brace of foxes.

He asked for it to be brought to him whereupon he took a poker, knocked the lid off the box and with a shout let the foxes out into The Lion Hotel, much to the consternation of the landlady and her female friends. It was an expensive joke as the animals broke bottles, glasses and crockery.

Mad Jack's life was described as a 'series of suicide attempts' and no more so than when he was driving a carriage or a four-horse gig. He tried to jump a tollgate and drove round the country roads of Shropshire without any regard for his own safety or any of the other road users.

Apperley said when Mad Jack was taking a new companion for a ride one day in his gig and the passenger remonstrated about his speed, Mytton asked if he had ever been in a gig that had been turned over. 'No,' the man replied, 'thank God, I have never been upset in one.'

'What!' cried Mytton, 'what a damn slow fellow you must have been all your life!' He promptly drove the gig up a bank at full speed tipping himself and his passenger out.

Even guests to his Shropshire home were not immune from his practical jokes. When an Oswestry parson and doctor left his house on horseback one evening after dining there, Mad Jack put on a highwayman's outfit plus mask and pistols and caught up with them at the edge of his estate.

He burst out on them shouting: 'Stand and deliver' and fired the pistols over their heads. Mytton took great glee in telling how they had galloped for their lives with him hard on their heels.

At another dinner party at Halston Hall he put on his hunting gear and arrived in his drawing room on his pet bear Nell which, when he tried to make it go faster, bit his calf. When Nell later attacked a servant Mad Jack had it killed.

He hardly treated his family any better. He had married his first wife, a Baronet's daughter, in 1818 but she died in 1820 and his second wife Caroline Giffard ran away in 1830. They bore him in total six children whom he would affectionately toss into the air as babies and pelt with oranges.

In the end, even for Mytton, who could drink eight bottles of port wine a day with a helping of brandy, the money began to run out. At first creditors couldn't find a bailiff prepared to take the risk of arresting 'Mad Jack', but in 1830 he fled to France to avoid his creditors, prison and court.

After a couple of years he decided to return to England and ended up in the King's Bench debtors' prison in Southwark, London, where he died in 1834 aged just 38 years old.

Ironically, Mytton's name lives on in Shropshire and abroad. There is a Jack Mytton Way, a long distance bridleway for riders, mountain bikers and walkers that runs for 116 kilometres/72 miles through South and Mid Shropshire.

There is a pub named after him at Hindford, Wittington, near his country house at Halston Hall; and a Mad Jack's Bar at the Mytton and Mermaid Hotel, Atcham, where his funeral cortege halted on its way to the chapel at Halston.

There is also a Mad Jack's Restaurant and a Mad Jack's Delicatessen in St Mary's Street, Shrewsbury, just up from The Lion Hotel.

However, one tradition does not survive. In 1999, nude students at the University of Minnesota campus in the USA held the annual Jack Mytton Run on the first class day after the spring break, which continued for ten years before police stopped it in 2009.

11

DISRAELI'S BITTER ELECTION CAMPAIGN

Many MPs have used The Lion Hotel as their political base, with the most famous being former Prime Minister Benjamin Disraeli, who was MP for Shrewsbury from 1841 until 1847. Just before the election, he stayed at the hotel and wrote to his wife, the extremely wealthy widow, Mrs Wyndham Lewis, whom he had married two years earlier, that it was not a restful time adding: 'The canvassing is more severe from eight in the morning to sunset.'

The canvassing was certainly severe. The voters of Kent where Disraeli had been elected MP in 1837 didn't want him to be their candidate again because they expected to be rewarded for their support and Disraeli hadn't paid all his bills.

In those days, Shrewsbury had two MPs, so when Disraeli was offered the Conservative nomination, he gratefully accepted it.

Disraeli was born in London to Jewish parents on December 21, 1804, but was baptised an Anglican when he was he was 12. He wasn't highly educated having gone to neither a private school nor university. So he was articled to a solicitor, but he didn't enjoy law, preferring to spend his time as a philanderer, a dandy and gambling on the Stock Market where he lost heavily.

His past was seized upon by his political Liberal opponents who accused him of abusing Parliamentary privilege by standing for Shrewsbury to avoid bankruptcy and imprisonment.

The *Shrewsbury Chronicle* quoted local solicitor William Yardley asking: 'Who is this Benjamin Disraeli? Why everybody knows him. Jews and gentiles. Saints, sinners and creditors know him . . . and he has once been trusted but not more than once.'

Disraeli's lifestyle of fancy clothes, European travel, the London social scene and his home in Buckinghamshire were costly for someone whose only income was from writing, as MPs were not paid then unless they were members of the Cabinet.

MPs were expected to provide free drinks and to pay to attend public dinners. Fortunately for Disraeli, his father, who paid his debts on at least three occasions, and his wealthy wife, helped him.

Anonymous election posters appeared around Shropshire questioning his suitability and honesty. When Disraeli travelled to Shrewsbury with Sir Philip Rose, a close friend and political adviser, they passed a huge poster on the side of a roadside barn which said: 'Judgment debts of Benjamin Disraeli, Tory candidate for Shrewsbury.' It then proceeded to unfold a long list of creditors and the amounts due to them. Disraeli peered at the poster and then said to his friend: 'How accurate they are. Now let us go on.'

Crowds taunted him with anti-Semitic cries of Shylock and waving pieces of roast pork on sticks at him. One heckler arrived with a cart telling Disraeli: 'I have come to take you back to Jerusalem.'

They also threw rotten eggs at him as he was addressing electors outside The Lion Hotel and stones were hurled at him while he was holding a meeting in The Square.

Disraeli hit back at his opponents, producing his own broadsheet in which he said: 'Utterly false, gentlemen, this is my clear and unequivocal reply to the dastardly attack which has been made on me. An attack, I should think, unprecedented for its malignity, its meanness, even in electioneering circles.'

Shrewsbury solicitor, William Yardley, replied by challenging Disraeli to a duel, which was prevented by the mayor who bound them both over to keep the peace.

□ □ □

The *Shrewsbury Chronicle* report in their edition of Friday, July 2, 1841, just days after the election on Tuesday, June 29, showed how bitter the campaign had been. It said:

The Tory party, knowing the unpopularity of their cause, with the great body of inhabitants, had provided sufficient means to carry their unconstitutional and nefarious design into full operation. The harpies of corruption were immediately let loose, and a large sum of money raised from the purses of the aristocracy was entrusted to the agents of 'dirty work'. These worthies immediately commenced their task and, during Monday evening, many conversions, almost miraculous, were effected. And that nothing might be wanting to ensure success, the zealous spouse of Mr Disraeli, escorted by the luminary Job Hunt, set forth on a visit to half-and-half and wavering tradesmen, whose consciences proved to be as elastic as the goods in which they dealt.

Promises made to the Liberals of one vote, with expressions of regret that both could not be given, were soon forgotten. And, at a private levee, held by the lady (Mrs Disraeli) that night at The Lion Hotel, numerous fallen spirits were honoured with an interview, which ended in their being converted to the faith of taxation and monopoly by a method never dreamt of in holy writ.

Whilst this backstairs influence was going on, a scene occurred in the public streets of the town, hitherto unparalleled in electioneering history, as such as we trust, for the honour of mankind, will never happen again.

A few partisans of the Liberal cause, who with more zeal than discretion, were exulting in the result of the nomination when 20 hands to one were in favour of Sir L Parry and Mr Temple, suddenly became the object of a ferocious and almost murderous attack in Barker Street.

A band of thieves and bullies from Birmingham, who had been specially hired for the occasion, and brought over by Wilding, a butcher, on the Sabbath, were instantly let loose on the crowd. An indiscriminate attack ensued; the friends of the Whigs and innocent lookers-on were immediately struck down by bludgeons and instruments nicknamed 'life preservers' and when their victims were on the ground, blows and kicks were inflicted without regard to life. The street became covered with blood, similar to a slaughterhouse, whilst from the adjacent windows raised the shrieks of agonised females who witnessed the sanguinary attack. Several persons were taken up half dead, and whilst the outrage was at its height, John Eddowes, the only representative of the loyal and religious class, was seen to applaud the scoundrels in their attack and, at the conclusion, lead them to a tavern to reward them with drink. For the truth of this, we can appeal to numerous witnesses who have given us their names.

Such was the closing scene of Monday (the day before the election). During the night, the emissaries of corruption were not idle, and the fruit of their labours was perceptible after the first hour of polling.

The unbought supporters of the Queen and Ministers did their duty nobly, but the lavish expenditure of Tory gold and unnecessary consequences of intimidation soon became apparent.

Among the most discreditable and disgusting derelictions of principle was the appearance in the political arena of several ministers of the Gospel of peace – ordained and otherwise – who scrupled as not to answer the question as to the change of residence allowed by the Reform Act, without the slightest regard to veracity.

On Wednesday morning, the Mayor made the usual official announcement at the hustings, after which the successful candidates, (Liberal George Tomline won the second seat) were placed in a carriage decorated with blue and white silk, drawn by six grey horses.

A number of banners and flags were carried in front; one having the motto *God protect the Church* was borne by a gentleman adorned with two black eyes. The vehicle and the retinue in the rear was guarded by a posse of Birmingham and Wolverhampton gentlemen.

After parading the town, the procession halted at The Lion, where the assembly were addressed (from the balcony) by their honourable representatives.

At the conclusion of their harangues, Mrs Disraeli was introduced to the crowds by Mr Burton, and her successful canvass was rewarded by reiterated cheers.

We are informed that Mr Disraeli wrote off to Sir R Peel, at the close of the poll, announcing his return. Whether it was done with a view of obtaining a snug birth in the event of the slippery Baronet obtaining office, in order to enable Benjamin to pay his debtors, time alone will develop.

The *Chronicle* concluded: 'But the agents of corruption and intimidation, and their unfortunate dupes, may rest assured that a long interval will elapse before they will have the opportunity of bartering their consciences for filthy lucre or delusive promises.'

That wasn't the end of the problems for the newly-elected MP for Shrewsbury. As Disraeli dined with Sir Baldwin Leighton at Loton Park, a mob gathered at Frankwell to attack him on his way home. Disraeli heard about this and stayed on a couple more days there before returning to London.

The defeated Liberals hadn't finished yet and launched election petitions to unseat Disraeli, accusing him of intimidation and 'the lavish expenditure of Tory gold'.

But after nine months, and because two Liberals at Gloucester were facing the same problem, a gentleman's agreement quietly dropped all the election petitions.

Disraeli was able to return to Shrewsbury in safety and it is recorded that he and his wife attended a ball at The Lion in 1843.

Although Disraeli won the Parliamentary seat, he did not get a seat in the Cabinet and with it a salary, though it wasn't for a lack of trying.

He wrote to Sir Robert Peel, the new Prime Minister, suggesting that he would make a good government minister. Peel disagreed and Disraeli stayed on the backbenches where he became a critic of the Conservative government.

Disraeli, who after six years as MP for Shrewsbury had moved to the Buckinghamshire seat because it was nearer his home, did eventually join the

Cabinet. He became Chancellor of the Exchequer three times in 1852, 1858 and 1866 and Prime Minster twice in 1868 and 1874, before retiring from politics in 1880.

However, he obviously won many people round in Shrewsbury for his work as their MP because when he died on April 19, 1881, the town's flags flew at half mast and its tradesmen closed their doors as a mark of respect.

12

SHOP WORKERS' FIFTY-YEAR BATTLE

IT IS AMAZING TO LOOK BACK at the history of The Lion and to see what effect it had on Shrewsbury.

A meeting held at the hotel on Thursday, January 10, 1861, was to make a profound difference to the conditions of shop workers in the town.

A campaign for shops to close at lunchtime on Thursday with a paid half-day holiday began with a letter to the *Salopian Journal* on November 7, 1860, appealing to the 'ladies of Shropshire' to use their influence to obtain early closing on Thursdays when the Volunteer Corps drilled.

Local historian Marjorie Dunham explained that the Volunteer force had been raised in 1859 when it was feared the French might invade England.

During the next two years, 18 groups of volunteer rifle corps were formed in Shropshire. Two of them, the 1st Corps and the 17th, had headquarters in Shrewsbury and later became the 1st and 2nd Shropshire Volunteer Battalions of the King's Shropshire Light Infantry. The list for the 1st Shropshire Volunteer Corps had 130 names, including 29 railway company clerks, workers from the Post Office, banks and the Inland Revenue, 14 solicitors, a barrister, five engineers, four gentlemen, two bankers, two school teachers, a dentist, a farm worker and the railway superintendent – but not one shop worker.

Numbers had increased rapidly in 1860 throughout Britain with 70,000 Volunteers by February that year, and 200,000 by November.

Patriotism and the chance to wear a uniform were two of the attractions to encourage the Volunteers to join up, but the main one was the social side with bazaars, dinners, fetes, an annual camp in July, a ball in February and a county rifle competition at Hawkstone Park. Up to 30,000 travelled on special trains to Wem for the first shooting contest held on June 28, 1861, at which Lord Hill, the Lord Lieutenant of the county, paid for the food and drink for the 1,200 Volunteers.

Newspaper reports said the tables groaned under the weight of the huge joints of meat and the Volunteers were able to help themselves to as much Hawkstone ale as they wanted, while picnics of pigeon pies and pasties, lobster salad, sherry and champagne were held all over the park.

It was probably fortunate the shooting contest began at 12 noon before the ale was served.

One journalist reported: 'Never has such a sight been seen in Shropshire before, and we fear it will be many a long day before such a one will be seen again.'

The Corps wanted even more of the working class recruits who were happy to volunteer if they could be given the time to attend the drills on Thursday afternoon, and so the campaign was born.

The *Shrewsbury Chronicle* wrote: 'In the annals of the country, no public movement has ever been received with such unbounded and universal sympathy.'

On November 23, 1861, the paper published the stirring letter of their columnist Rifleman who said:

> The subject is not new, but never before has the occasion presented itself so rife with hopes of a successful issue as the present offered by the Volunteer Rifle Movement and the necessity of time for drill. Even the most antiquated prejudice should give way to this national movement for the defence of England. It is not the bubble of an hour. England is no longer a nation of shopkeepers, but a nation of heroes. The assistance of every Englishman and Englishwoman is needed to perfect the movement. A half-holiday would give greater vitality to it. This is a remarkable age. Progress is the rallying cry of Genius and we must go on with the time or stand still and be trampled upon.

Following the letter a group of young men drafted a circular to be sent to ladies in Shrewsbury, which led to the forming of the Half-Holiday Association, believed to be the first of its kind outside London.

The Rev Charles Wightman, vicar of St Alkmund's, argued that for people working 12 hours a day, six days a week a half day's paid leave was not too much to expect adding: 'Let the ladies dispense with the drapers on Thursdays from 1pm to promote the Volunteers.'

Another letter writer said the half-holiday would lead to better observance of the Sabbath, which because of long hours, was now 'wasted in idleness and its necessary accompaniment, sin'.

In early December 1860, the Half-Holiday Association announced that they were holding a meeting on Thursday, January 10, in The Lion Assembly Room.

The Mayor and Corporation appealed to shop owners to allow their employees time off on Thursdays to drill with the Volunteers; the clergy urged employers to meet before the date of the meeting while the editor of the *Chronicle* said in his paper: 'Our correspondent Rifleman has been nobly answered by the ladies. The movement has met with success beyond the hopes of the most sanguine.'

The paper even asked the young men why they wanted to become a Volunteer. One replied in the paper: 'To be a Volunteer has become a *sine qua non* of a young man's life. All other amusements are insipid after this. Even the good old manly game of cricket pales before the fiery ardour of the wish to be a rifleman. Even the quietest, most unassuming young man has in him the stuff of which England's heroes are made.'

However, not everyone agreed. The Vicar of Holy Trinity, Shrewsbury, the Rev Colley, spoke against early closing from his pulpit, fearing that the young would misuse the free time and that 'temptations to evil were furnished by additional hours of leisure'.

The next day the much-heralded meeting took place at The Lion with the Hon. Mrs Henry Burton in the chair.

Robert Slaney, MP, proposed the half-holiday from 1pm on Thursdays in the mutual interest of employers and the employed, which was seconded by the Rev Yardley of St Chad's. The Rev Charles Wightman proposed that the ladies sign a pledge not to shop on Thursday afternoons, which was seconded by Captain Cholmondeley. Finally, Captain Calvert proposed that a committee of ladies should canvass traders, asking them to sign an agreement to close at 1pm from Thursday, February 7 and Captain Salt, one of 14 solicitors present, seconded this.

The *Chronicle* was jubilant at the success of The Lion meeting, saying it had been 'a union of talent rarely met with – the ladies, the influential, the clergy, dissenting ministers and Volunteers and it was a notable achievement for Charles Hutchinson, the chairman of the Half-Holiday Association.'

The paper's columnist, Rifleman, wrote to say he had retired from the movement which was now in better hands.

But the battle was far from over. When the employers met at the George Hotel on January 18, Alderman Edward Hughes, a wine merchant, took the chair and said it was monstrous that traders should be dictated to when they should get up and when they should go to bed.

Mr Heath, a Pride Hill tailor and outfitter to Shrewsbury School, said the class of men he employed would rather work more days in the week, if it were possible, than to have a half-holiday.

After much debate, a majority of 14 carried the following proposition.

Whilst most desirous of affording those in our employ, especially such as have already joined or are wishful to join the Volunteer Corps, every opportunity for drill or recreation conducive to health and well-being, no disrespect to the ladies, whose kindly feeling prompted them to join agitations in favour of the half-holiday, but whose sympathies there is every reason to believe enlisted mainly by incorrect representations leading to erroneous impressions as to its desirability, as well as to the ultimate results, if adopted, this meeting views with feelings of regret and indignation the advertisement which has this day appeared in the *Shrewsbury Chronicle* and signifies the most decided opposition to the movement as calculated to produce most injurious effects upon the trade of the town.

The advertisement, which had caused such offence, was drawn up by Charles Hutchinson and said:

HALF-HOLIDAY IN SHREWSBURY

We the undersigned being most anxious and desirous of securing to the young people of Shrewsbury a weekly Half-Holiday on Thursday afternoons, hereby pledge ourselves 1) not to shop on Thursday afternoons; 2) not to permit our domestics to do so; 3) not to countenance those tradesmen who endeavour to take advantage of that half-day by keeping open their houses of business!

The traders were upset by the second and third resolutions, which they thought meant that ladies would not shop at all at establishments which did not close for the half-holiday. The association immediately withdrew the second and third pledges.

The battle continued to rage in the letters columns of the papers and on January 30, an employer revealed that a compromise of a 4pm closure had been agreed.

On February 1, a notice in the *Chronicle* under the heading 'An Earnest Requisition from the Ladies of Shrewsbury', and signed by 84 traders, argued that 'with proper regulation of business the youth could be spared for moral, intellectual and physical improvements from 4pm on Thursdays'.

However, some who signed pointed out they would close only if other shops did.

In 1862, the Government announced that no more Volunteer companies were to be formed, which suggested recruitment was no longer a problem.

By 1880, company drill for Volunteers in Shrewsbury now took place at 7.30pm with recruits being given uniforms after 30 drills and soon the Volunteers had no connection to the Half-Holiday Movement.

In 1886, the Shop Hours Regulation Act limited the number of hours for under 18 year olds to 74 hours per week, but some shop assistants were still working 12 to 16 hours a day.

However, it was not until 1911 that legislation finally guaranteed a half-holiday beginning at 1pm – 50 years after the campaign was launched in Shrewsbury at The Lion Hotel on January 10, 1861.

13

THE LION PLAYS ITS PART IN HELPING FORM SHREWSBURY TOWN FC

MANY SHREWSBURY TOWN FANS are probably unaware of the part The Lion Hotel played in helping form their football club.

However, on page seven of *The Eddowes Shropshire Journal* of May 26, 1886, the paper's columnist, Athlete, reported: 'A meeting was held at The Lion Hotel, Shrewsbury, when it was agreed to re-start the once well-known club, the Shrewsbury Town Football Club.'

He continues: 'As there is some talk of the Castle Blues giving up, it is confidently expected that the new-old club will command a strong list of fixtures. The honorary secretary is Mr A W Lloyd, of 102 Frankwell, and he will be glad to receive applications for fixtures.'

Athlete concludes: 'It is to be hoped that this new organisation will at least be able to make as good a show in cup ties and friendly matches as the Blues did, without gaining the unenviable notoriety which the old club revelled in.'

However, there was one slight problem. On page four of the same edition of the paper there is a report which states: 'Shrewsbury Town Football Club: A meeting was held on Thursday night at the Turf Hotel, Shrewsbury, to re-start this well-known old club.'

It is probable that both accounts are true as Mike Jones, in his book, *Breathe on 'em Salop: Official History of Shrewsbury Town F.C.*, says: 'The two main sporting hostelries of the time (1886) were the Lion and the Turf (Claremont Hill). The Shropshire FA meetings were held in The Lion, while several sides used the Turf as a base. This may explain why the reports in the local press about the formation of the club differ.

'It is eminently possible that both reports are based on fact, and that an early get-together at The Lion moved on to the Turf to finalise details with the potential playing strength. Either that, or the club was initiated on a pub crawl.' It might well have been a class thing. Mike later refers to a headmaster, a solicitor and a gentleman who was secretary of the Flower Show, adding: 'These gentlemen would probably have been at the meeting at The Lion, before joining up with their future team-mates at the Turf.'

To show how sport has changed over the last 125 years it is interesting to quote Athlete's advice to Shrewsbury Town FC in his column after he had reported the founding of the new club.

He writes:

Footballers may be assured that they will add not spark to their lustra by rough play, and though such tactics may, and often do, please a certain section of the spectators, there can be no doubt that prestige is irrevocably lost by what Major Marindin, who is so well known all over this sporting county of ours, so justly describes as un-English.

It not only deserves perhaps this rather harsh sounding verdict. But it is quite beneath any football player to resort to roughing.

If nature has blessed you with a giant's strength, use it only as a giant when doing good work. To knock those about who are weaker than yourself, just because it has so happened that you are opposed to them in a game requiring strength, nerve and skill, is indeed a cowardly pastime and all who indulge in it should be scouted from out of sight of the ground. So Shrewsbury Town Football Club, you have my blessing. May you prosper and raise the town more in the eyes of leatherchasers by sending up a team to compete in the final for the National Football Association Challenge Cup of 1886-87.

Although Aston Villa won that year's FA Cup beating West Bromwich 2-0 in the final, Shrewsbury Town did indeed prosper.

After playing friendlies and regional cup competitions for a few seasons, Shrewsbury Town were founder members of the Shropshire & District League in 1890-91 before joining the Birmingham & District League in 1895-96, where they were league champions in 1922-23.

In 1910, the club moved to a new ground, Gay Meadow, just down from The Lion Hotel by the English Bridge over the River Severn where they stayed for 97 years until moving to a new out-of-town stadium on Oteley Road in 2004

In 1937-38, the club joined the Midland Champion League where they had a very successful first season. They did the league and cup treble scoring 111 goals, and won the Welsh Cup after a replay, as well as the Shropshire Senior Cup.

After being Midland League champions in 1949-50, Town were admitted to the old Division 3 (North) of the Football League in 1950, where they played in all three of the lower tier leagues.

Town went on to be champions of the Football League Third Division (third tier) in 1979 and stayed in the Second Division (second tier) for ten years until being relegated. They then topped the Football League Third Division (fourth tier) in 1994, although they were relegated out of the Football League into the Conference in 2003. However, they bounced back at the first attempt when they won the Conference play-off final in 2004.

But it was the cup where Town prospered and they had many famous victories.

They were semi-finalists in the Football League Cup in 1961, Welsh Cup winners on six occasions and quarter-finalists in the FA Cup in 1979 and 1982.

The Lion has continued to team up with Shrewsbury Town and support the club throughout its history, with many of the visiting teams staying at the hotel.

One memorable occasion was the third round of the FA Cup in 1979. The flamboyant football manager, Malcolm Allison, and his Manchester City team stayed at The Lion when they played Shrewsbury Town in what turned out to be the local team's most memorable season, reaching the last eight of the FA Cup and winning promotion. In fact Town drew with Wolves in the quarter-final, and were actually in the draw for the semi-final: Arsenal v Wolves or Shrewsbury.

'Manchester City came into The Lion before the game very confident and full of themselves,' said the then hotel banqueting manager, John Holding.

But he added: 'After the game they left the hotel very quickly and very crestfallen after losing 2-0 to the Town.'

14

GHOSTLY GOINGS-ON

EVERY HISTORIC HOTEL HAS ITS OWN GHOST STORIES and The Lion Hotel is no exception. Shrewsbury's Town Crier, Martin Wood, tells of five ghost stories in his book *Haunted Shrewsbury*.

The lady in blue

Leading from the rear of the hotel up to the Adams style ballroom is a curved staircase and several guests have seen a Victorian lady dressed in a powder blue dress standing at the bottom of the stairs waiting for someone.

She eventually gets fed up and turns to walk away. Although there used to be a door, there isn't now and she walks through a wall which is part of a cloakroom.

Some years ago, a young night porter went to the garages late at night, and when he returned to the main building, he walked past the lady in blue. Without saying a word he went immediately to the reception desk, grabbed a piece of paper and wrote: 'I quit.'

He walked out of The Lion and never came back inside the building again!

The lady in blue is never seen outside the hotel. Was she a victim of a coach and four that caught her as she walked out of the hotel in a huff as tradition suggests?

Mystery pianist

Towards the end of the 20th century, the hotel was playing host to a world famous pianist, who had sent his personal tuner to ensure everything was ready for the concert.

The tuner sorted out the piano and the hotel staff were told not to even breathe on the instrument in the Ballroom.

In the early hours of the following morning the young night manageress was very angry to be awoken by the sound of music played by a first-class pianist.

She peered over the edge of the balcony and asked, not very politely, who on earth was playing.

Then she looked closer and saw that the lid of the piano was still closed, but the music continued.

The manageress immediately went back to bed – and spent the rest of the night under the duvet absolutely petrified!

Sealed up room

Above the curved stairs is a small room that has been sealed up. Many years ago, it is believed something terrible occurred in the room and the staff would never go there on their own, so the manager decided to have it bricked up.

Even then, moans could be heard coming from the room and a lit candle would sometimes be seen in the window. Now even the window has been sealed off.

The basement ghosts

The extensive basement of The Lion is very old, with some of it dating back to the 18th century. In one part there are two rooms, which according to legend, were used as a small chapel. In one of these rooms have been seen the ghosts of two ladies in prayer.

Shock for chef

The outside of St Julian's Church, built in 1750, was originally very plain with the red walls separated from the main street by a row of houses. In one of the houses had lived old John Tarbuck, a well-known shoemaker, who kept a diary in the 1780s.

He said: 'One Assize time, the Judge's cook, who was staying at The Lion, fell ill.' Tarbuck said Mr Taur collapsed after a choking fit one evening and a doctor was called who pronounced him dead and signed the death certificate. As he had no living relatives, they buried him immediately in a grave at St Julian's behind Tarbuck's house.

That evening as he and his niece were sitting by the kitchen fire they heard a muffled sound of groans and struggles coming apparently from behind the fireplace. They began listening but the sounds soon ceased.

One story says that other people had heard screams and that when they dug Mr Taur up the next day they found the underneath of his coffin lid had been scratched and his fingers had been worn away.

It turned out that the chef had only fallen into a coma and that he had woken up in his grave. He is probably the only person in Shrewsbury to be buried twice in the same grave!

- Ghost tours around Shrewsbury, usually in October and November, can be booked through the Tourist Information Centre on 01743 281200 or visitorinfo@shropshire. gov.uk or privately with Martin Wood on 07718951902.

15

THE LION – ROARING INTO THE TWENTIETH CENTURY

A T THE START OF THE 20TH CENTURY, Queen Victoria was still on the throne and in Shrewsbury life hadn't changed too much for many years.

The county of Shropshire was then made up of small, often isolated villages and a few bustling market and industrial towns. The roads were still rough tracks in many areas and cars were a rarity, until after the First World War.

Only local industries had electricity on a small scale, while homes were lit by candles, oil lamps and gas lights with water coming from a well, pump or stream and where the toilets were an earth closet with a bucket inside.

It was also a fairly quiet time for The Lion, relying on the locals and the railways to fill its rooms. The owners bought the lease for the site in 1910, then the freehold in 1920.

In the late 1920s, as local directories show, The Lion finally absorbed all the property lying between it and Henry Tudor House (74-75 Wyle Cop) adding a new wing and also building at the back of the hotel.

However, it was not until the 1930s as people began to travel wider that The Lion became more popular and well-known.

In 1936, in the List of Hotels, Boarding and Apartment Houses, issued by the Town Clerk, it proudly reported that The Lion had hot and cold water in all bedrooms. Bed and breakfast ranged from 9 shillings and sixpence (47.5p) to 10 shillings and sixpence (52.5p) depending on the choice of room.

Those who wanted to spend a week at The Lion could do so for £5 and 5 shillings (£5.25).

Due to its strategic position at the top of Wyle Cop, it continued to play a part in the annual town events, such as the Shrewsbury Carnival, which still continues each June. Ruth Cooke was the daughter of Leonard Cooke, who farmed at Grange Farm, Bicton, and who used to deliver the milk to The Lion Hotel before the Second World War.

As Leonard knew the chef he was invited one evening in the summer of 1939 to take his six-year-old daughter into what is now known as the Dickens room, and watch the Shrewsbury Carnival procession come up Wyle Cop.

'As it was before the war and the dark years that followed there was no restriction on light,' said Ruth who went on to become a Land Girl and then a history teacher at Shrewsbury High School.

'I remember the intense excitement as up to 20 floats drove slowly up the Cop and the Carnival Queen waved graciously to the crowds.

'I can still see the scene now,' said Ruth. 'It was the most exciting event in my life to that date, and it was for some time to come.'

A coup for The Lion Hotel in 1940 was when the Grand Lodge of the Royal Antediluvian Order of Buffaloes (RAOB) decided to hold its national conference there.

The Order is defined as a Fraternal, Benevolent and Social organisation in the United Kingdom, open to any male over the age of 18 provided he is a 'true and loyal supporter of the British Crown and Constitution' and that he 'enters of his own free will and consent'.

The brochure given to delegates, which can still be seen at Shropshire Archives in Castle Street, Shrewsbury, said: 'We welcome you to the historical town of Shrewsbury, of which this little souvenir will give you some idea of its attractiveness, and sincerely hope that, despite the dark clouds that obscure our national horizon at this present time, your stay will nevertheless be enjoyable.'

It continued: 'We are immensely proud of the honour of entertaining the Grand Lodge in Shrewsbury for 1940.

'Although a small province in Buffaloism, we nevertheless pride ourselves on being great in striving to uphold the traditions of the Noble Order and all it stands for, which makes it so dear to the hearts of all of us.

'We trust your deliberations will further the interests and prosperity of the Order, despite the many disadvantages under which we are at present carrying on, and that the end of 1940 will find us doing our good work under happier and brighter conditions.'

It was signed by Bros L A Wright, F S Hicks, G C De Ruyter, C J Taylor, A G Beeton and D C Lowe.

During the Second World War, the Lion and the Raven Hotel were the top hotels in town.

The Raven on Pride Hill, which was a different hotel to the stagecoach inn, the Raven & Bell on Wyle Cop where Robert Lawrence had worked, had more than 100 American servicemen accommodated there.

By April 1943, it was made into an American Red Cross Leave Club whose motto was 'to give the boys a real good time' and they did that with cabarets and dances.

If the Raven had the Americans, then The Lion had the British with their top events attracting the local gentry and VIPs.

The Lion also had a more unusual role in the war. Due to its flat roof and prominent location it was used as a lookout for enemy aircraft.

After the war there was a shopping boom. The F W Woolworth store empire wanted to move into Shrewsbury and they put in a big offer for the Raven site which the hotel owners couldn't refuse. It closed on December 23, 1959, and an auction of its contents was held in February 1960.

Planning laws were much more relaxed then, but even so, many Shrewsbury people were horrified when the majestic building was demolished in June 1960 and a modern Woolworth store opened its doors on October 30, 1964.

Today the site is occupied by H&M stores, next to Marks and Spencer.

With its rival gone, The Lion enjoyed its unsurpassed position as the town's number one hotel as the austerity of the war years began to wear off in the 1950s and 1960s and the hotel began to step into another golden age.

16

DANCES AND DINNERS IN THE SWINGING SIXTIES

THE 1950S AND 1960S WERE SUCCESSFUL DECADES for The Lion and there were very few Saturdays when people didn't flock to the hotel for the popular dance nights or to enjoy one of the society dinners in the Ballroom.

One of those who enjoyed the social scene was Jancis Maloney who now lives in Chirbury, Shropshire.

Born in 1938 in Kent, Jancis and her family were evacuated to Exeter before her father was invited to become a modern languages master at Shrewsbury School. Living next door to a schoolboys' boarding house she found she had a ready made social life, and by the age of eight she was having dancing lessons at the school.

However, it was not until she was a 14-year-old at Shrewsbury High School, that she was invited to one of the top balls at The Lion, when one of her girlfriends had to drop out.

'I remember having to wear one of my cousin's cut-down mauve evening dresses with a sash and sleeves while my friends had pink and white strapless dresses. I also remember wearing my mother's stockings for the first time; which was a ghastly experience as they were so ticklish,' recalled Jancis.

'But the evening itself was excellent and The Lion Ballroom was done up beautifully for the dance.'

She was now on the dance circuit, and the holidays from just before Christmas until mid January were one long social whirl for the young teenager. Every year there were up to 15 dances with at least three at The Lion.

'Our doormat on November 1 was covered with white envelopes inviting us to dances all over the town,' said Jancis. 'But the grandest ones we wanted to go to most were those at The Lion, which included an orchestra as well.'

Fortunately, she had an aunt in America who designed patterns for a clothing firm and Jancis received a steady stream of ball gowns through the post.

'There were usually up to 100 at the dances and they were always well controlled with parents there as well. We also drank dilute Claret Cup,' Jancis added.

She said one of the other advantages was that the dances led on to many other social invitations to walks, sport and cinemas.

'We didn't pair off so soon as they do nowadays,' said Jancis, 'we were just one big social group.'

Jancis remembered her younger brother, Tim Ewing's 18th birthday at The Lion. But by then she was 21 and studying English and ethics at St Andrew's University in Scotland and she was about to marry Michael Maloney, a chemistry master at Shrewsbury School, whom she met through Scottish dancing. Her brother's birthday was the last dance at The Lion for Jancis and the start of a new family role.

☐   ☐   ☐

Another person who remembers the Saturday night dances organised by Bert Dann to the music of Don Gilbert and his band was John Holding.

But he saw it from a different viewpoint, he was a member of the hotel staff.

Born in Oakley Folly, at Loggerheads, near Market Drayton, John first came to Shrewsbury to work for £2 10 shillings (£2.50) in 1954 as a 15-year-old apprentice chef at the Raven. He had always been impressed by the town as his father and uncle had brought him to the Flower Show each year since he was six.

'I had always enjoyed making meals, but when I chose cooking classes instead of metalwork at Market Drayton Secondary Modern School I was teased unmercifully,' recalled John.

However, his training stood him in good stead. Within two years he was moved on to the management team, where his first job was to look after the Prime Minister, Harold Macmillan, who was spending three days at the hotel for a visit, which included a Shropshire ploughing match.

'The security was nothing like today,' said John. 'The party of six included a private secretary and only a couple of security people. My job was to ensure that every aspect of their stay went smoothly, but I had to do it discreetly and stay in the background.'

Within two years John was out of work when the Raven was sold and for three months he couldn't find a job until he was offered the very humble position of 10th porter at The Lion in 1958.

'In those days, apart from the weekends, The Lion was just a glorified travellers' hotel,' said John, 'mainly used by commercial travellers staying a night or two during the week.

'The hotel was very dowdy, the reception was right by the front door and the manager's office was a bit of a jamboree. There was no lift and everything had to be carried by hand up to the rooms, including lugging huge barrels of beer up the George III staircase to the Ballroom. In those days there was even a gents only bar in a back room.'

The porters had to stand on the reception steps to await the visitors.

John and the other staff lived in a block of 20 rooms at the back of the hotel which were sparsely furnished and where the only space for clothes was behind a curtain.

Another person who remembers those days at The Lion fondly was Kenneth Clinton, who was born in 1941, the youngest of nine children to a blacksmith and his wife at Hungerford, Craven Arms.

'I enjoyed cooking but I didn't dare tell them at school in case I was teased for being a sissy,' he recalled. He worked in the village bakery before joining The Lion as a commis waiter in 1957. Having eight brothers and sisters it was luxury for him having his own room in the staff block with hot and cold water. Kenneth was paid £1 10 shillings (£1.50) for a six-day split-shift week from 8am to 3.30 and back on duty at 6.45pm, finishing any time between midnight and 1am. 'You didn't dare count the hours,' he said.

Kenneth, who is now living in Ludlow, left The Lion and went to Quaglino's in London returning to Shrewsbury when he was 22 to become head waiter for a year, before moving on to a number of hotels and restaurants in the county.

'I really enjoyed my two stints at The Lion, they were a welcoming team and it was good training.'

Guests were given a warm welcome with roaring fires everywhere and a beautiful hand-carved bar which was later sold to an American and shipped out to the United States.

However, life for the hotel staff improved in the early 1960s when Rocco Forte, the son of the owner Charles Forte, ordered a big facelift for the hotel.

The place was redecorated, a lift was installed, new furniture was brought in, the workers' accommodation block was upgraded, pictures were put up on the walls and an extension was built increasing the number of bedrooms from 45 to 62.

☐   ☐   ☐

John Holding's life at The Lion had also improved. Within three months he had been moved up to third porter and two years later he was Head Porter.

He was promoted to wedding adviser and then banqueting manager, where he was working 80 hours a week and sleeping in at the hotel as he oversaw the big increase in dinners and dances in the Ballroom.

He recalled the military balls and dinners where the silver cutlery, china plates and candelabra were brought in from the barracks. Then there were the dinners for the hunt balls, the Ladies Circles, the Rotary Clubs, the Law Society, the Licensed Victuallers' Association, the tobacconists and the Burns Night dinners where John had to bring in the haggis. But the highlight for many was the County Architects' ball, a real social occasion as Shrewsbury-born Gerald Cattle, who now lives in Minsterley, recalled.

Born in 1941, he joined the Shropshire County Council Architects Department as a 20-year-old architectural assistant in 1961. In those days, there were three drawing offices with ten architects in each office as there were many school building projects as well as designing the new Shirehall.

'Most of the architects were real party animals and every day two car loads would go to The Lion for lunch,' said Gerald. 'But the high point of the year was the County Architects' Ball, a black tie and posh frocks do that was always a sell-out as all the support staff and architects from the private practices in the town would be there.'

He said the drawing offices would take it in turns to produce the menu, the table plan and entertainment with each trying to outdo the previous year.

He said the most memorable year was 1963, just after the Americans had put a man in space. A huge rocket was constructed in sections about 5ft by 2ft rather like a box kite with a light timber framework covered in thick paper with fins, a pointed nose cone and all painted white with USA in large black letters.

The stunt was done in great secrecy and on the day of the ball it was taken to The Lion and put up against the balcony.

'After the dinner and an hour or so of dancing, the lights were dimmed and spotlights lit up the rocket,' said Gerald. 'One of the architects appeared on the balcony in a silver space suit with helmet to loud cheers. He appeared to enter the nose cone and on a simulated lift-off special CO^2 fire extinguishers were released at the base producing a dense white cloud. The fixing at the nose cone to the balcony was then released and the rocket toppled over on to the dance floor and when the sections parted balloons were released.

Gerald said no work was done for about a week, with all the planning for the ball. 'I could not imagine anything like that happening in a local authority today,' he added. 'But this was the start of the Swinging Sixties and after the long, grey years following the war the whole nation seemed up for a bit of sport.'

At the same time as these out of the world balls and banquets were taking place there was a new type of guest coming to the hotel as families arrived for a bargain weekend break.

John Holding, who used to travel to London and throughout the Midlands talking to the coach firm operators to persuade them to come to Shrewsbury, said some days there were six coach loads of holidaymakers coming to The Lion for lunch before travelling on to Wales in the afternoon, while some evenings there were two coach loads of people staying overnight.

For John there were the many memories from that era. For example:

- The three-day John Player conference where girls in mini skirts were continually giving out cigarettes.
- The Shrewsbury School speech day where parents would stay at The Lion for the weekend, attending a concert at the school put on by the pupils on the Friday night, followed by the speech day on the Saturday afternoon. John said he used to earn more those weekends as a porter than he did as the banquet manager, and often received £40 of tips to add to his weekly porter pay of £50 a week.
- The annual August Shrewsbury Flower Show was another huge occasion, which brought in visitors from all over the country, and there wasn't a room free for miles around.

However, it wasn't just the posh events at the Lion that hit the headlines. John helped put on classical concerts in the Ballroom, which was decorated with flowers from the Percy Thrower Garden Centre while country and western evenings were held downstairs. They were all so successful that the *Shrewsbury Chronicle* dubbed him Mr Showbiz of Shrewsbury.

After 25 years, John was rewarded with first class rail tickets to Forte Hotel's Quaglino's in London where he was presented with a gold watch and his long-service award. When he retired two years later in 1985 he received an engraved tray.

'One of the town's building society managers said in a speech in The Lion Ballroom that I was the sergeant major of the banquet department,' said John.

'I took that as a great compliment. I wanted the running of every banquet to go smoothly and I wanted every diner to remember it as a great evening.'

In those days, the head waiter at The Lion always wore jacket and tails plus white gloves, while the porters wore maroon jacket and trousers and they were not allowed to take their ties off, no matter how hot the weather was.

He added: 'I was brought up on hotel etiquette and I still think it is important today.'

17

ROLLING OUT THE RED CARPET FOR POP STARS AND TV STARS

THE LION'S GROWING REPUTATION WAS SPREADING nationwide and many famous celebrities were now choosing to come to the hotel. Kenneth Clinton remembers the most famous group of all coming to Shrewsbury in 1963.

- The Beatles 'were walking upstairs in The Lion past a decorator who wolf whistled at their Beatles haircut and called out "hello darling",' recalled Kenneth. 'John Lennon turned to him and said "Wack, we are worth much more than you" and carried on up the stairs.'

Kenneth also recalled meeting Benny Hill with his 'much greased hair', actor Felix Aylmer, and English rose grower Harry Wheatcroft who was in Shrewsbury for the Flower Show and who 'was dressed very flamboyantly with an open neck shirt'.

John Holding also met many of the stars providing with him with a host of memories. Here are a few of the stars he met.

- Pat Phoenix, alias Elsie Tanner from the TV soap Coronation Street, who 'was a lovely lady'.
- Peter Adamson, alias Len Fairclough in Coronation Street, 'stayed in his room drinking.'
- Comedian Tony Hancock 'was not a nice man'.
- Hughie Green and Monica Rose, stars of the ITV show *Double Your Money*, stayed a week and accepted an invitation to attend the hotel staff party. 'Hughie Green was a giant of a man, so tall and so nice. He signed the inside of the handbags of the hotel ladies staff saying "Hughie Green was here".'
- Morecambe and Wise played at the Granada (now a bingo hall below Shrewsbury Library). 'They lived quite separate lives even though they were in the same hotel. I remember the *Shrewsbury Chronicle* photographer taking them up to the Ballroom where they set up a fun picture with their reflections in the mirrors.'

Sycamore House, the octagonal building at the rear of The Lion Hotel, was left by owner John Ashby in his will to his wife, and it can still be seen today. It was sold in 1779 for £1,000 to Shrewsbury stationer John Bishop to help pay off Ashby's debts.

An advertisement bill promotes a grand concert given by Signor Niccolo Paganini at The Lion Hotel on Thursday, August 15, 1833. The programme hangs in the entrance to The Lion today. [Picture: Richard Bishop]

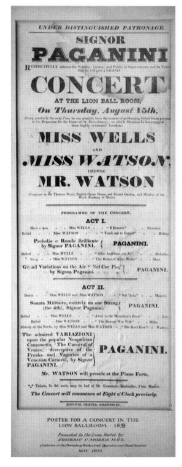

An advertisement in the Birmingham Gazette dated May 7, 1787, for the Shrewsbury Mail Coach.

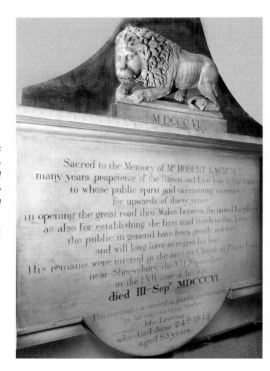

The tombstone inside St Julian's Church of Robert Lawrence who brought the stagecoaches and prosperity to The Lion Hotel at the end of the late 17th and early 18th centuries.
[Picture: Richard Bishop]

The Saxon church of St Julian's has many links with The Lion Hotel nearby.

Shrewsbury School. Charles Darwin was educated here before the school was moved to the other side of the River Severn. Notice the Darwin statue in front of the building which is now the town library.

This picture hangs in the entrance to The Lion and shows the Shrewsbury Wonder arriving at the hotel. Interestingly the four horses are white, not the black horses which Sam Hayward insisted on picking up from the Mytton and Mermaid at Atcham for the final journey up Wyle Cop to The Lion. It is believed the artist and the then owner of The Lion fell out over the fee for the picture and the artist's revenge was to leave the horses white. [Picture: Richard Bishop]

Shrewsbury Unitarian Church. Charles Darwin attended and preached here.

Looking down Wyle Cop from The Lion Hotel in 1930. [Picture supplied by David Trumper]

- Radio DJ Diddy Dave Hamilton 'loved staying in the Dickens suite'.
- Pop singer Adam Faith performed for two nights at the Granada, and when news got out that he was staying at The Lion, teenage girl fans gathered at the front door and John had to lock it and let Adam out through the back. Another memory was when he took the pop star's luggage up to the room. 'I turned round to look for him and there he was doing cartwheels down the corridor.'
- TV personality and Jim'll fix it presenter Jimmy Savile stayed at The Lion while he was on a charity bike ride from Land's End to John o'Groats. 'He was really nice, just as he appears on TV.' When they asked him to sign the new visitors' book on the first page he signed diagonally across the whole page with 'Hi, Jimmy Savile was here'.
- Pop singer Lulu arrived at The Lion with a sore throat and asked for some honey and lemon to be brought up to her room as she was due to sing at the Music Hall. 'When she opened her door I was shocked to see she was topless. I was more embarrassed than she was, but Lulu was unperturbed and invited me in telling me to leave the drink on the table.'
- Radio and TV personality Lady Isobel Barnett used to stay at the hotel when she joined the famous shooting parties on the Berwick estate. 'I was given a brace of pheasant one time.' John said he also remembered a group of Lancashire cotton men who every year would come back hungry after a busy morning shooting and order steak and kidney pie with chips.
- Pop group Cliff Richard and the Shadows arrived to play at the Granada. 'I had to press Cliff Richard's trousers and I remember Hank Marvin asking for a cheese and onion sandwich to be taken up to his room.'
- Kenny Ball and his Jazzmen came to play for Judge Michael Manders' 40th birthday in the Ballroom. 'It was fun to see all the judges dancing away.'
- Frankie Vaughan stayed when he appeared at the Granada.
- Singer Helen Shapiro wanted a taxi. 'I ordered a lovely limousine. When she saw it she said she wanted a cab, so I had to explain to the driver that Helen Shapiro didn't want him.'
- Actress Hattie Jacques 'was a lovely lady.'

Pam Williams, who is the present front of house manager at The Lion, has worked at the hotel since 1976 in two stints. She has met a number of stars and remembers:

- Actor Martin Shaw, who is probably best known for playing Ray Doyle in

The Professionals. 'He liked having breakfast in his room and he was so good looking all the female staff used to fight over who would take the food up to him.'

- Irish actress Gemma Craven stayed for a fortnight at the hotel. 'She loved Shrewsbury's small shoe shops and every day she went shopping and came back with a new pair of shoes which she showed to all of us on reception.'
- American jazz vocalist Curtis Stigers came to The Lion with his wife and child. 'He was always so polite.'
- Author, broadcaster and former MP Gyles Brandreth played at Theatre Severn and stayed at The Lion. 'He was charming, just like he is on TV.'

Pam also remembers meeting musician Jools Holland and Emmerdale star Matt Healy, who played the part of Matthew King and appeared in pantomime in Shrewsbury.

Another staff member who recalls stars at The Lion is Gary Harrigan, a taxi driver in Shrewsbury who worked at the hotel from 1988-96, firstly in the maintenance department and then as a kitchen porter and night porter.

'As a 16-year-old I had no interest in the hotel's history at all, but the longer I worked there the more interested I became,' said Shrewsbury-born Gary who is now married with two children.

- He remembers seeing Ian Woosnam, the professional golfer who was born in Oswestry, the 'Crafty Cockney' and world darts champion Eric Bristow, world snooker champion Ray Reardon, actor John Inman best known for his role as Mr Humphries in the TV comedy *Are you Being Served?* and Sandi Toksvig, the comedian, author and broadcaster.

But it wasn't just TV and pop stars who came to The Lion.

- The Welsh FA used it for their meetings and it was where they interviewed future managers of the Welsh team and where the successful candidate was announced to the waiting press and TV cameras.

However, there were more serious occasions when big names arrived at the hotel.

- Racing driver Stirling Moss gave a press conference at The Lion after being found guilty at Shropshire Quarter Sessions of driving a 'Baby' Austin dangerously at Chetwynd, near Newport, on September 29, 1960. He was fined £50 and had his licence suspended for 12 months.

'The place was packed, and what upset me most was that some members of the press stood on a lovely carved chest to get a better view,' said John.

- Politician Enoch Powell, who had made controversial speeches about race relations in Britain, spoke in the ballroom. 'The security for that evening was amazing.'
- But there were some lighter moments. Every year since 2003, the town has hosted the Shrewsbury International Cartoon Festival, which has attracted around 40 full-time, professional cartoonists and caricaturists from the UK and abroad, including Australia and Canada, all of whom stay at the Lion.

'It is always great fun having them here,' said Pam Williams. 'They set up their boards around the hotel and did caricatures of everybody, including the staff.'

18

BACK TO THE FUTURE

OVER THE LAST FOUR CENTURIES, LIFE HAS GONE FULL CIRCLE at The Lion Hotel. In 1780, the new independent owner Robert Lawrence took over the hotel and restored it to its former glory.

In 2006, independent owner Howard Astbury bought the hotel and is now restoring it as a reminder of its glorious past.

Running inns and hotels is in Howard's blood. Born in 1944 in Bridgnorth, he was brought up in the Clee Hills where his parents ran the Old Miners' Arms at Hopton Bank in south Shropshire. Locals used to call it the Lady's Finger, as Howard's mother, Edith, who looked after the pub for 32 years, used to wave a finger at any of the regulars if they misbehaved or used bad language.

Even as a schoolboy at Cleobury Mortimer, Howard ran bars at local dances to earn some pocket money before he went to train as an electrical engineer for the National Coal Board at the nearby Highley Colliery. But 18 months after he qualified, just after his 22nd birthday, the colliery was closed, so Howard decided to go back to what he knew best, hotels.

He joined Grand Metropolitan Hotels as a trainee running the Harte and Garter in Windsor for just under 10 years. Then in 1976, he bought his first hotel, the Old Bell in Warminster, a historic coaching inn that had closed down. He married while he was there in 1979 and now has two grown-up children, Louise and Nicholas.

At the same time as Howard was modernising the Old Bell, The Lion was also being updated.

In October 1984, the Shrewsbury hotel underwent a £270,000 facelift which included £70,000 on restoring the restaurant which now, for the first time for many years, has a separate entrance on to Wyle Cop, and £150,000 on upgrading the bedrooms, while in July 1991 new kitchens were built.

In February 1984, the hotel restaurant hit the local press when restaurant manager John Cushion linked up with Condover School for the Blind to produce one of the first ever Braille restaurant menus for visitors.

Finally, the hotel turned its attention to its two famous lions. In August 1996, a telescopic crane was brought in from Mold, Wales, and it took two and a half hours to lift the three-quarter ton of lion at the back of the hotel so workers could repair the deteriorating plinth which the owners feared might one day crash through the roof into the Ballroom below.

A few years later the lion over the main doorway at the front was re-gilded. The event was watched by John Brown, of Highfields, Shrewsbury, a lecturer in the teaching and practice of painting and decorating, who said it took 23 books with 25 squares of 24-carat gold leaf worth £20 each to complete the task.

Meanwhile, after turning round the Old Bell's fortunes, Howard bought the Ilsington Country House Hotel on the edge of Dartmoor in 1992 and then in 2001, the modern Exeter Court Hotel in Devon.

But his heart lay in Shropshire and in historic hotels, so when The Lion Hotel came on the market in 2006, he decided to buy it, even though the only times he had come to Shrewsbury previously was to visit three aunts.

'I didn't have a passion for modern hotels like the one in Exeter and there was no pride in ownership,' said Howard. 'But I knew of The Lion's reputation and with it being a town centre hotel it had an all-year round clientele whereas the Devon hotels were very seasonal, busy in the summer but very quiet in the winter.'

Howard bought the hotel from the Regal Hotel Group who in turn had acquired the hotel from Granada, formerly part of Trust House Forte, in May 1996.

One of his first tasks was to improve the roof, renew the electrics and buy new beds.

'People often don't realise how many improvements go on behind the scenes,' said Howard, who then concentrated on redecorating the 59 bedrooms, sprucing up the ground-floor area and upgrading the restaurant.

Many of the rooms are named after Shropshire people and include the Darwin, Dickens, Pickwick, Paganini, Lind Room and Clive rooms. There's also:

The Thrower Room – Percy Thrower was Shrewsbury's Parks Superintendent from 1946-74 and his responsibilities included the famous Dingle in the centre of the town's Quarry. He has been described as Britain's first celebrity gardener appearing on the BBC's Gardening Club in 1956 and then the BBC's *Gardeners' World* from 1969-76.

The Sidney room – Sir Philip Sidney, who was born in 1554, attended Shrewsbury School from when he was nine until 13. He became a prominent poet, courtier and soldier.

The Owen room – Wilfred Owen was the First World War poet, who lived at

1 Cleveland Place and then moved to Mahim, Monkmoor Road, Shrewsbury. He died on November 4, 1918, just one week before the Armistice. His name is commemorated in Shrewsbury Abbey and there is a memorial in the churchyard.

The Peters room – Ellis Peters was the pseudonym for Shropshire born Edith Mary Pargeter who wrote the popular *Brother Cadfael* medieval mystery novels set in Shrewsbury, many of which were filmed for television in the 1990s.

The Webb room – Mary Webb was a Shropshire born English romantic novelist and poet in the early 20th century, whose books are set in the county.

To increase the number of guests, Howard marketed the hotel through the internet to encourage the more discerning guests who had previously stayed at The Lion to return now it was back under private ownership.

This has been successful and Howard worked next on improving the Hayward Restaurant. In February 2011, he employed award-winning Michelin chef Ian Matfin, who has worked for Gordon Ramsey at the Aubergine Restaurant in London; Raymond Blanc at Le Manoir aux Quat' Saisons, Oxfordshire, and Michael Caines at Gidleigh Park Hotel, near Newton Abbott, Devon.

Aiden Byrne, who worked at The Dorchester, London, and received his first Michelin star at the age of 22, is Consultant Chef. He had met Ian on the TV programme, *The Great British Menu.*

'We want to ensure The Lion is known for fine dining, fine service and a fine stay and is up with other top hotels such as The Chester Grosvenor,' said Howard.

Next he is turning his attention to the historic Ballroom in the Grade 1 listed hotel, which is used for wedding receptions, parties, functions and occasional concerts by Shropshire Music Trust.

'The challenge is the room needs real restoration work by experts as the shutters have had layers of paint added over the years while the plasterwork has lost some of its detail,' added Howard.

Once the hotel is completely restored he wants to spend more time marketing The Lion and Shrewsbury.

'We need to promote the history of the town and the hotel more,' he said. 'I still go to different parts of the county and they look blankly at me when I mention Shrewsbury and its historic past.

'I am looking forward to seeing the town and the hotel regain their place back in the history of Britain,' he said.

Howard's dream is that it may again be said of The Lion, as it was in 1817, 'No house upon any of the great roads between Holyhead, Bath, Cheltenham, Bristol, Liverpool, Manchester, North and South Wales stands in higher estimation having a constant influx of the first families in the kingdom.'

APPENDIX I

If you have arrived at The Lion for your stay, explored the hotel and looked at its history, what else is there to do in Shrewsbury and the surrounding area?

The Visitor Information Centre in the Shrewsbury Museum & Art Gallery in Rowley's House, Barker Street, Shrewsbury, 01743 281205, www. shrewsburymuseums.com is the best place to start for a complete list of all the town attractions plus their opening times.

The following, in alphabetical order, provide some ideas to explore Shrewsbury:

Bear Steps Gallery, Fish Street, near the Prince Rupert Hotel, is a 15th Century Tudor timber hall showing exhibitions of painting, photography and crafts.

Coleham Pumping Station, a Victorian building in Longden Coleham, houses two massive restored steam-drive beam engines.

River cruises on the Severn depart from the Victoria Quay, near the Welsh Bridge.

St Alkmund's Church, near The Lion Hotel and behind St Julian's Church, is an 18th century church with a medieval tower and an unusual painted glass window.

St Chad's Church, near The Quarry, is an unusual and elegant round church built in 1782.

Shrewsbury Roman Catholic Cathedral in Belmont, which can be seen from the back of The Lion, was designed by A W Pugin and opened in 1856.

St Julian's Church, which is only 100 metres from The Lion, dates back to the 12th century. Inside there is the tombstone of Robert Lawrence, and although the church is closed, visitors who wish to see inside should ring the owner, Andrew Wright, on 01743 353516.

St Mary's Church, up the hill from The Lion via Dogpole to St Mary Street, is a medieval church with a wonderful collection of stained glass windows from the 14th to 19th centuries.

Shrewsbury Abbey, just down Wyle Cop from The Lion and on the other side of the River Severn and the English Bridge, is a Norman abbey, the site of the first English Parliament and the setting for the Brother Cadfael mysteries.

Shrewsbury Town FC play league football at the Greenhous Meadow, on Oteley Road.

Theatre Severn is close to the Welsh Bridge and Frankwell.

The Music Hall at the back of the Square is being refurbished and will open as the new home for the County Museum and Art Gallery and Visitor Information in the summer of 2012.

The Old Market Hall is an Elizabethan building in the Square now used as an arts venue and café.

The Quarry is a 29-acre riverside park with a stunning sunken flower garden, The Dingle, designed by Percy Thrower.

Just outside Shrewsbury

Attingham Park, three miles south east of the town on the B4380, is an elegant 18th century mansion owned by the National Trust with Regency interiors and a deer park landscaped by Humphrey Repton.

Battlefield, two miles north of the town off the A49 Whitchurch road, is the site of the Battle of Shrewsbury in 1403, with an exhibition, farm shop and café.

Haughmond Abbey, two miles north of the town, off the B5062 Newport road, is an Augustinian Abbey owned by English Heritage.

Wroxeter Roman Vineyard, four miles east of the town, off the B4380, is one of the world's most northerly vineyards.

Wroxeter Roman City (Viroconium), four miles east of the town, off the B4380, was the fourth largest city in Roman Britain and is owned by English Heritage.

Further afield

Hawkstone Park and Follies at Weston-Under-Redcastle is an historic parkland in 100 acres created in the 18th century by Sir Rowland Hill and his son Richard.

Ludlow Castle is a fine medieval ruined castle in a fascinating town.

Much Wenlock is where in 1850 local surgeon William Penny-Brookes (1809–95) introduced physical education into British schools and inspired the forerunner to the modern Olympic Games. The Wenlock Olympian Society holds its own Olympics in the town every July.

Shropshire Hills Discovery Centre in School Road, Craven Arms, is Shropshire's only grass-roofed public building and explains the geological, historical, archaeological and cultural significance of the Shropshire Hills.

Stokesay Castle, near Craven Arms, is one of the finest and best preserved medieval manor houses in England.

APPENDIX II

The list of trades people and creditors involved in the re-building of The Lion, from 1775–78, gives a fascinating glimpse into all those involved, plus their costs. As well as carpenter and joiner William Haycock, whose details are given in chapter 2 and whose bill came to just over £2,698, other people included:

- John Tudor, of Shrewsbury, who supplied bricks.
- Joseph Bromfield, who was the mayor of Shrewsbury from 1809-10 (owed £132), supplied lime for the plasterer which was delivered by Thomas Peck of Wenlock (another creditor).
- Shrewsbury craftsman and plasterer Joseph Bromfield, whose separate charges for decorating the Lion Inn, as well as Ashby's house in Milk Street, was £341. He was still owed £132.
- John Nelson and his partner Richard Lee (owed £316) did the masonry work.
- Shrewsbury craftsmen Arthur Richards and John Betton oversaw the glazing.
- Robert Hill, plumber, also of Shrewsbury, whose bill was £475 and who was still owed £275.
- Painter Edward Podmore (owed £114).
- Other Shrewsbury tradesmen who supplied furnishings to The Lion included tradesman John Lloyd; cabinet makers Richard France and Tennant Lacy; brazier White Cooke; upholsterers William Davies and John Newling; ironmonger James Winnal; joiner John Thompson and stationers John Bishop and Joshua Eddowes.

In September 1776 an oven boiler and other iron work was delivered by Samuel Darby of the Coalbrookdale Company, while in December 1778 a partition boiler, stove plates, grates and other items were delivered in December 1778, some months after The Lion had opened.

Another creditor was the Shrewsbury carrier Thomas Powell, who with his partner John Bather, claimed to be owed £83 for goods transported between July 1776 and January 1779, which was probably for the pair of lions and a vase that Ashby had ordered in May 1776 from The Strand in London firm of Parker and Harris which made casts. These were probably bas-reliefs, one of which was placed over the porch to the former dining room and still survives today.

APPENDIX III

In *Shrewsbury – A Heritage of Old Inns and Taverns*, Derek Row lists all the known former landlords at The Lion which he has kindly allowed to be reprinted here.

Robert Lawrence 1780–1806
William Tomkins 1807–28
Ann Bassnett 1840
Edward Lewis 1849–56
George Curtis 1861
Augustus Lucas 1863
Mrs Frances White Horn 1870
Sarah Roberts 1876–78
Charles Fleet 1882–85
William Tompkins 1888
John Southern (manager) 1889–1903
William Walter Southern 1903–04
Robert Cordell 1904-07
Grace Elizabeth Roberts 1907–12
Ida Lottimer Latimer 1912–14
Frank George Jenkins 1914–15
Ethel Budden 1915–17
Sarah Williams 1917–20
Hayward Luther Randells 1920
Henry Kane O'Kelly 1920–26
Albert Crighton Baxter 1926–30

Harold Bounds 1930–33
William R Craig 1930–39
Henry Nelson Snook 1939–46
Frank Milson Hutchinson 1946–52
D Carter 1952–53
W F Phills 1953–54
G E McSellers 1954–58
R G Farrer 1958
G H Farrer 1958–61
M R Jones 1961–63
Paul Heerch 1963
Ian Walker Manser 1975–77
Douglas Edward Goodall 1977–79
Michael Stevens 1979–81
Thomas Duffurn 1981–84
Mayhew Thomas Solomonson
   1984–96
Kevin Herbert 2001–2
Kate Jordan 2002–6
Howard Astbury (owner)
   2006–present

REFERENCES

To help me in my research I have used the following books and publications:

Bill Champion, *Shropshire History and Archaeology, Transactions of the Shropshire Archaeological and History Society*, Vol LXXV 2000.

Brian Haughton, *Coaching Days in the Midlands,* Quercus.

Charles G Harper, *The Holyhead Road* (The Mail Coach Road) in 1902.

Edward Corbett, *An Old Coachman's Chatter*, London 1890.

Fisher's *Annals of Shrewsbury School.*

George Kay, *Royal Mail*, Central Press.

Howell Rees, *The Famous in Shrewsbury.*

Jrschina Williams-Karesch, *Shrewsbury: A Biography.*

Julia Ionides, *Thomas Farnolls Pritchard of Shrewsbury.*

L C Lloyd, *Inns of Shrewsbury.*

Laurin Zilliacus, *From Pillar to Post* (Heinemann).

Martin Wood, *Haunted Shrewsbury*, History Press.

Mike Jones, *Breathe on 'Em Salop: Official History of Shrewsbury Town FC.*

Nathaniel Hawthorne, *English Notebooks*, London 1883.

Nigel Hinton and David Trumper, *Historical Hostelries.*

Nikolaus Pevsner and John Newman, *The Buildings of England, Shropshire.*

Notes in *Salopian Shreds and Patches* 1878.

Owen H and Blakeway JB, *History of Shrewsbury*. London 1825, Vols 1 & 2.

Philip Leason, *Stone Historical and Civic Year Book.*

Piggott and Co (publishers), *Directory of Shropshire*, 1829, 1835.

Robert Southey, *Letter from England*, published in 1807.

Sally Bevington, *Shropshire Life*, May 2010; www.shropshire.greatbritishlife.co.uk

Samuel Bagshaw, *Gazetteer and Directory of Shropshire* (Sheffield, 1851).

Shrewsbury Chronicle.

Shropshire Notes and Queries, Vol. V, page 49.

Steve Booth, 'The Golden Age of Coaching', *Stone Historical and Civic Year Book.*

T Auden, *Shrewsbury*, 2nd edition, London 1923.

The Victorian Shrewsbury Research Group, editor Barrie Trinder, *Victorian Shrewsbury.*

Thomas De Quincey, *Confessions of an English Opium-Eater*, 1862.

The Buildings of England, Shropshire, (Yale University Press).

Toby Neal, *Shropshire Since 1900: A Year by Year News History.*

Vivien Bellamy, *The Making of Shrewsbury*, Pen & Sword Books Ltd.

W T Palmer *The King's Highway* Vol XII, No. 1 January 45.